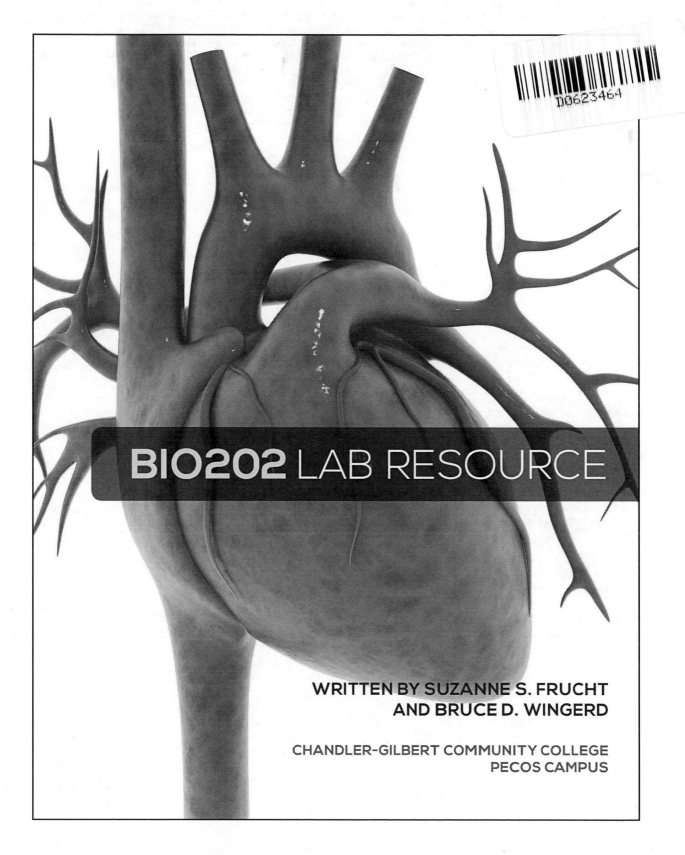

BIO2O2 LAB RESOURCE

WRITTEN BY SUZANNE S. FRUCHT
AND BRUCE D. WINGERD

CHANDLER-GILBERT COMMUNITY COLLEGE
PECOS CAMPUS

bluedoor
flexible & affordable learning solutions™

Chief Executive Officer: Jon K. Earl

President, College: Lucas Tomasso
President, Private Sector: Dawn Earl
Director of Operations and Strategy: Michael Schafer

Print Solutions Manager: Connie Dayton
Digital Solutions Manager: Amber Wahl
Developmental & Production Coordinator: Rhiannon Nelson
Senior Project Coordinator: Dan Woods
Senior Project Coordinator: Peggy Li
Project Coordinator: Erica Rieck
Project Coordinator: Jessie Steigauf
Project Coordinator: Nicole Tupy
Production Assistant: Stephanie Larson

Cover Design: Dan Woods

ISBN-13: 978-1-68135-022-6

© 2015 by bluedoor, LLC.

© Cover images by Shutterstock.

Published by bluedoor, LLC
      10949 Bren Road East
      Minneapolis, MN 55343-9613
      800-979-1624
      www.bluedoorpublishing.com

Printed in the United States of America.
10 9 8 7

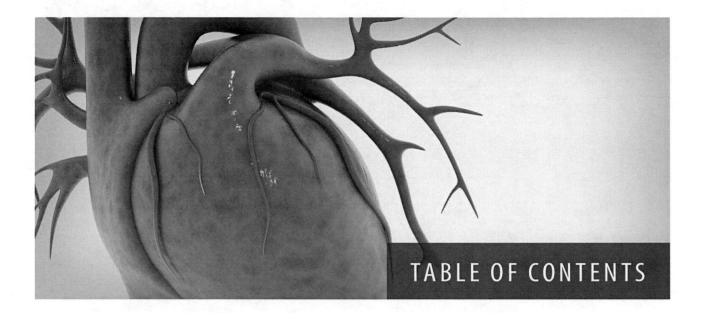

TABLE OF CONTENTS

LABORATORY SAFETY POLICY
REVISED, SPRING 2015
BIOLOGICAL SCIENCES DIVISION
CHANDLER-GILBERT COMMUNITY COLLEGE

ATTIRE AND BEHAVIOR

Students, faculty, and laboratory personnel shall,

a. wear hard-soled shoes covering the whole foot

b. wear safety glasses/goggles, disposable gloves, masks (when instructed to do so), and aprons/ laboratory coats during exercises in which microbes, glassware and chemical reagents are handled or when dangerous fumes may be present

c. not apply cosmetics (make-up, lip balm, etc.) in the laboratory

d. wear disposable gloves when handling preserved specimens

e. not light a Bunsen™ burner (or equivalent) near a gas tank or cylinder, leave open flames unattended, or move a Bunsen™ burner when lit

f. not wear loose, long hair, and/or loose clothing, when working near an open flame or incinerators

g. turn off the gas jets when a Bunsen™ burner (or equivalent) is not in use

h. use caution and appropriate equipment when handling hot glassware and heated chemicals

i. report, to the faculty teaching the course, broken or malfunctioning equipment

j. report any condition appearing unsafe or hazardous

k. communicate to the faculty teaching the course if a procedure or directions are not clear, and understand it is his/her responsibility to ask the faculty for clarification

l. conduct themselves and communicate in a professional and respectful manner

FOOD AND BEVERAGES

Students, faculty, and laboratory personnel shall NOT,

a.   drink in the Pecos Campus Microbiology/General Biology laboratory room SAG – 108, nor in the Williams Campus Microbiology laboratory room ENGL 116

b.   drink from a container that does not have a screw top, and/or is not spill proof in laboratory rooms (Pecos Campus: SAG – 101, 103, 104, and 105; Williams Campus: ENGL 118, THOM 100, and 103) or preparation areas. Drink containers using straws shall not be allowed in any laboratory classroom or preparation area

c.   eat in any laboratory room or preparation area

d.   pipette anything by mouth

MICROORGANISMS

Students shall understand,

a.   working with live microorganisms entails risks including, but not limited to, contracting disease or infection and/or injury from laboratory equipment even when using nonpathogenic bacteria and fungi

b.   the risk of contracting infections and/or disease, which could be serious or even fatal, is significantly increased for individuals whose immunity is impaired for any reason

c.   persons with immune system deficiencies (including, but not limited to, those individuals undergoing chemotherapy, taking immunosuppressive drugs, {e.g., corticosteroids}, diabetes, autoimmune diseases {e.g., lupus or multiple sclerosis}, pregnancy, and/or being HIV positive) are at an increased risk of infection

d.   he/she suspects he/she has less than normal immune function, he/she should consult a physician as to the advisability of enrolling in biology at this time

CHEMICALS

Students, faculty, and laboratory personnel shall,

a.   understand working in a biology laboratory includes, but is not limited to, working with organic and inorganic chemicals that may or may not cause sensitivities

b.   read the **Material Safety Data Sheets (MSDS)**, identify the hazards, and understand first aid measures prior to using chemicals specific to a laboratory activity

c.   be aware of the location of the MSDS in the laboratory room or preparation area

d.   understand the risks of chemical exposures; if he/she suspects he/she has a chemical sensitivity then he/she should consult a physician as to the advisability of enrolling in biology at this time

LABORATORY CLEANLINESS

Students shall,

a. thoroughly clean laboratory table-tops, before and after class with disinfectant, and wash hands after all laboratory periods

b. keep walkways clear of backpacks, books, purses, etc.

c. clean and disinfect microscopes, before and after laboratory activities, and return them to the proper location

d. return models, and other equipment used during laboratory activities, to the proper location

e. wash and dry dissection tools and return them to the proper location *facing the same way in the tools tray*

f. dispose of urine specimens (if personal urine is used) in the restroom toilets

g. return goggles used during laboratory procedures to sterilization goggles cabinet and faculty shall lock and turn it on at the end of the class period

h. not pour chemicals back into containers unless instructed to do so

i. not operate equipment until instructed in its use

Students, faculty, and laboratory personnel shall,

a. thoroughly wash hands after handling preserved specimens

b. dispose of preserved specimens in the dissection waste container

c. not put chemicals in the sink or trash unless instructed to do so

d. dispose of sharps in the sharps container

e. dispose of blood and/or contaminated waste material in the hazardous waste container

CHEMICAL SPILLS, GLASS BREAKAGE, AND ACCIDENTS

Students shall,

a. properly clean up broken glassware and dispose of it in the broken glass container

b. properly clean up chemical spills and dispose of waste as instructed

c. immediately report glassware breakage, slide breakage, chemical spills, and accidents to the faculty teaching the course

d. understand proper procedures for using the safety shower and eye-washing stations

Students, faculty, and laboratory personnel shall,

e.   administer first-aid, immediately, for bleeding, chemical spills, falls, etc.

OUTDOOR ACTIVITIES

Students, faculty, and laboratory personnel shall,

a.   use caution during any outdoor activities by being alert for snakes, poisonous insects or spiders, stinging insects, poison oak, poison ivy, etc., and water that may pose a hazard.

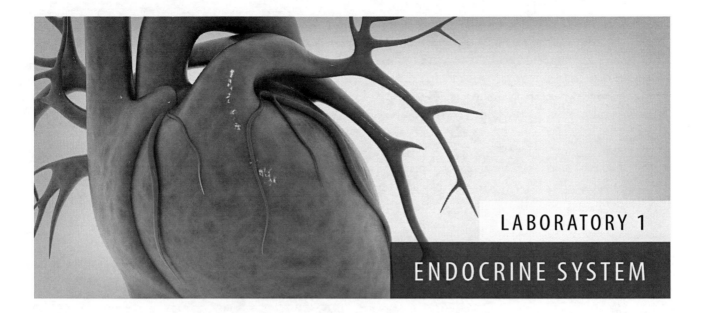

ENDOCRINE PATHOLOGIES

For an endocrine gland to secrete the correct amount of hormone, it must have some method to monitor the body's need for that hormone. Negative feedback loops are the most common method for accomplishing this. In a negative feedback loop a change in conditions away from the status quo, or **set points**, triggers a reaction from the endocrine gland that works to move body conditions back to the status quo. When status quo is reached, the trigger for action is gone and the gland stops secreting hormone. A good example is the reaction of the pancreas to blood glucose levels.

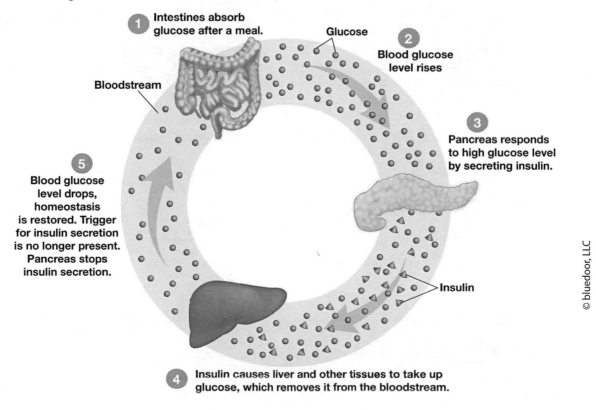

1 Intestines absorb glucose after a meal.

Glucose

Bloodstream

2 Blood glucose level rises

3 Pancreas responds to high glucose level by secreting insulin.

5 Blood glucose level drops, homeostasis is restored. Trigger for insulin secretion is no longer present. Pancreas stops insulin secretion.

Insulin

4 Insulin causes liver and other tissues to take up glucose, which removes it from the bloodstream.

© bluedoor, LLC

Diseases caused by endocrine gland dysfunction are most often recognized by the changes that occur in the target organ when there is too much or too little hormone. Conditions that result from too much hormone are **hypersecretion disorders**. An example is an endocrine gland tumor that secretes large amounts of hormone regardless of what the body requires. Conditions that result from too little hormone are **hyposecretion disorders**. This type of condition may develop if there is injury to the gland from trauma or when the body's own immune system attacks it (an autoimmune disorder).

▶ Below is a list of conditions that may be caused by either hypersecretion or hyposecretion of a hormone. Read the description of each condition, then match it to its hormone hypersecretion or hyposecretion in the second column.

_____1. diabetes insipidus – the kidneys are not able to reabsorb water when the body needs to conserve water

_____2. diabetes mellitus – there are high levels of glucose in the bloodstream

_____3. dwarfism – the bones grow too slowly, leading to a person who is short statured

_____4. gigantism – the bones grow too fast, leading to a person who is extremely tall

_____5. Hashimoto's disease – low metabolic rate, weakness, mental and physical sluggishness

_____6. hypoglycemia – low levels of glucose in the bloodstream, producing fatigue and fainting

_____7. pheochromocytoma – increased heart rate, blood pressure

_____8. Recklinghausen's disease – the bones lose calcium and blood calcium level is too high

_____9. tetany – low blood level of calcium, leading to muscle and nerve irritability

_____10. virilism – the appearance of male secondary sexual characteristics in a female

a. hypersecretion of growth hormone

b. hyposecretion of growth hormone

c. hyposecretion of antidiuretic hormone

d. hyposecretion of parathyroid hormone

e. hypersecretion of parathyroid hormone

f. hypersecretion of epinephrine

g. hyposecretion of insulin

h. hypersecretion of androgens

i. hyposecretion of T_3 and T_4

j. hypersecretion of insulin

Labeling Activity

▶ This figure represents the pituitary gland surrounded by the targets that its hormones affect. Use the clue given by the target to determine which hormone goes with each number. Fill in your answers below.

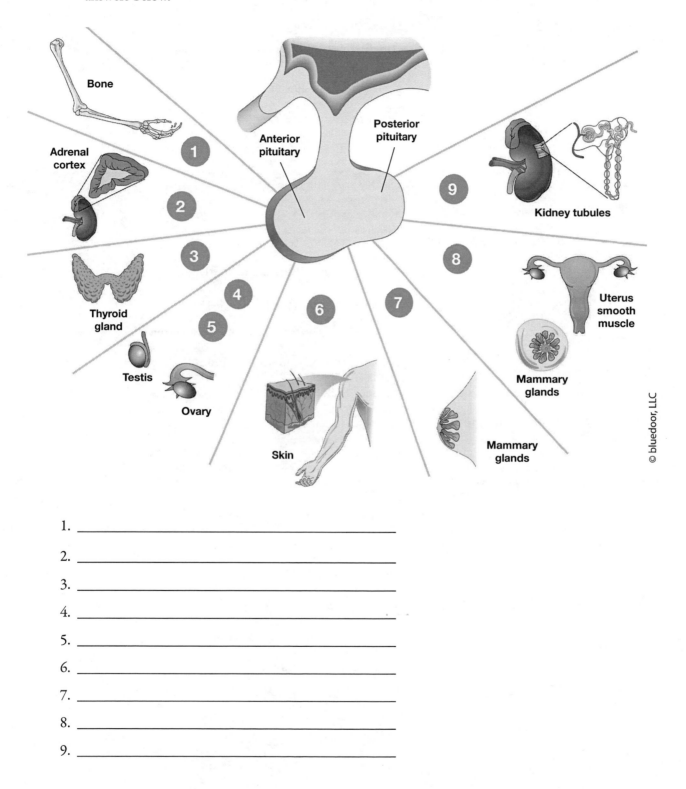

© bluedoor, LLC

1. _____

2. _____

3. _____

4. _____

5. _____

6. _____

7. _____

8. _____

9. _____

Key Term Matching

_____1. aldosterone

_____2. pituitary gland

_____3. alpha cells

_____4. thyroid follicles

_____5. epinephrine

_____6. hormone

_____7. thymus gland

_____8. parathyroid glands

_____9. interstitial cells

_____10. follicle-stimulating hormone

_____11. pancreas

_____12. thyroid gland

_____13. zona reticularis

_____14. hypersecretion

_____15. corpus luteum

_____16. parathyroid hormone

_____17. pineal gland

_____18. infundibulum

_____19. cortisol

_____20. parafollicular cells

_____21. circadian rhythm

_____22. adrenal glands

_____23. hyposecretion

_____24. beta cells

_____25. antidiuretic hormone

A. secretes progesterone

B. attaches pituitary gland to hypothalamus

C. secretes androgens

D. a butterfly-shaped gland

E. the body's 24-hour clock

F. condition of releasing too much hormone

G. raises blood calcium levels

H. a glucocorticoid hormone

I. also called clear or C cells

J. secretes melatonin

K. condition of releasing too little hormone

L. considered to be part of the lymphatic system

M. stimulates water reabsorption by kidneys

N. consist of an outer cortex and inner medulla

O. secrete insulin

P. contain colloid

Q. secrete glucagon

R. a chemical messenger

S. a "fight or flight" hormone

T. a mineralocorticoid hormone

U. stimulates development of ova and sperm

V. secrete testosterone

W. also called the "master gland"

X. both an endocrine and exocrine gland

Y. composed of chief cells

Coloring Activity

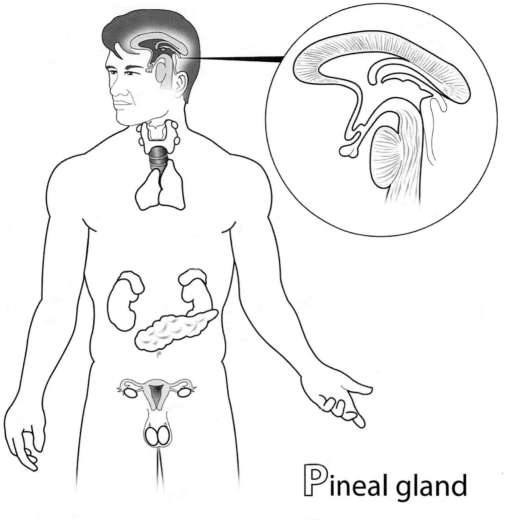

Pineal gland

Adrenal glands

Pituitary gland

Ovaries

Testes

Pancreas

Thymus gland

Parathyroid glands

Thyroid gland

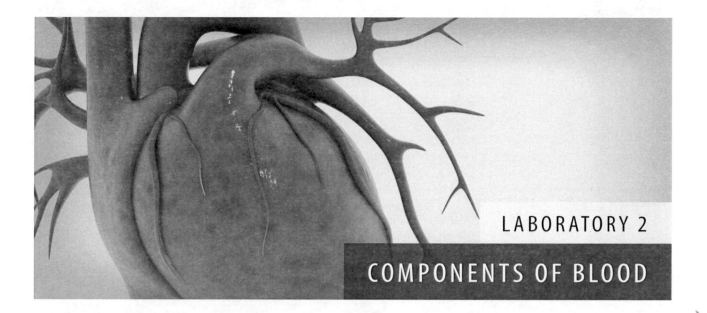

LEUKEMIA

Leukemia is cancer of the blood-forming tissue in bone marrow and lymphatic tissue characterized by uncontrolled production of leukocytes. The extremely large number of leukocytes then spill out into the bloodstream and eventually infiltrate other tissues of the body. Leukemia may occur as either acute or chronic. **Acute leukemia** is characterized by a rapid onset of symptoms and the abnormal leukocytes are primarily immature and non-functioning. **Chronic leukemia** has a more gradual onset and fewer immature leukocytes. Because these lymphocytes continue to function, the patient may initially be relatively symptom free.

Leukemia may develop in almost any type of leukocyte, but the two most common types are **myelogenous leukemia** and **lymphocytic leukemia**. The figure on the following page illustrates how the different formed elements, erythrocytes, leukocytes, and platelets, are all derived from a **pluripotential stem cell**. Pluripotential is a term meaning a cell has the potential to differentiate into two or more types of cells. The first differentiation of this pluripotential cell is into either a **myeloid stem cell** or a **lymphoid stem cell**. If a myeloid stem cell becomes cancerous, then myelogenous cancer develops. If a lymphoid stem cell becomes cancerous, then lymphocytic cancer develops.

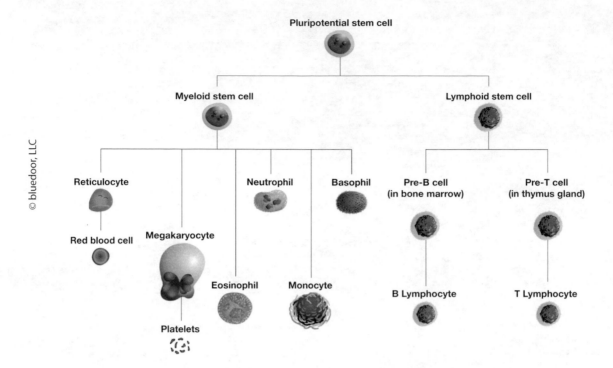

Pluripotential stem cell

Myeloid stem cell

Lymphoid stem cell

Reticulocyte

Neutrophil

Basophil

Pre-B cell
(in bone marrow)

Pre-T cell
(in thymus gland)

Red blood cell

Megakaryocyte

Eosinophil

Monocyte

B Lymphocyte

T Lymphocyte

Platelets

1. If a person develops acute myelogenous leukemia, what leukocytes may be involved and how mature are they in the bloodstream?

2. If a person develops chronic lymphocytic leukemia, what leukocytes may be involved and how mature are they in the bloodstream?

Common symptoms of all types of leukemia are caused not only by the poor functioning of leukocytes, but also by the loss of erythrocytes and platelets. These formed elements have a reduction in their number because the tissue that normally produces them is crowded out by the uncontrolled growth of the leukocyte-producing tissue.

For each symptom below, state whether leukocytes, erythrocytes, or platelets are involved.

3. anemia

4. easy bleeding

5. repeated infections

6. enlarged lymph nodes

7. shortness of breath

8. excessive bruising

Labeling Activity

▶ Write the name of each formed element in the blank and then match it to its photo.

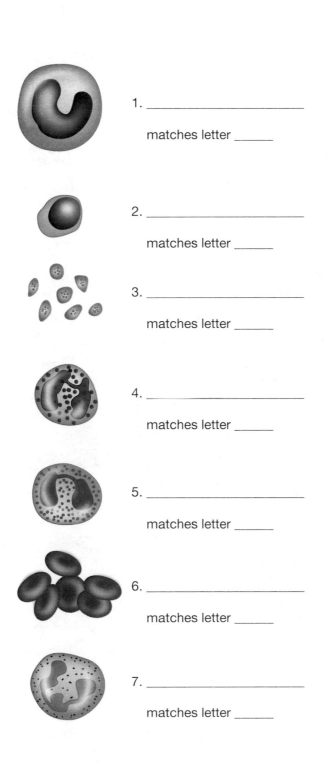

1. _____

   matches letter _____

2. _____

   matches letter _____

3. _____

   matches letter _____

4. _____

   matches letter _____

5. _____

   matches letter _____

6. _____

   matches letter _____

7. _____

   matches letter _____

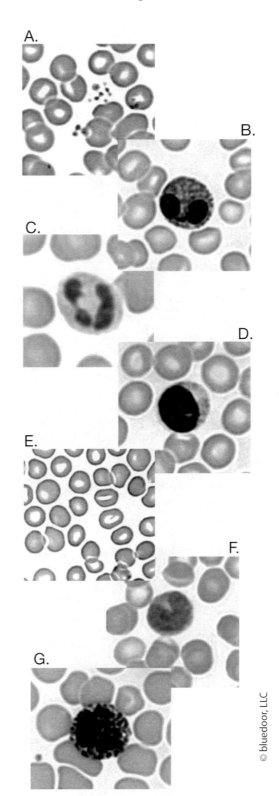

A.

B.

C.

D.

E.

F.

G.

© bluedoor, LLC

Key Term Matching

_____1. megakaryocyte

_____2. phagocyte

_____3. *eosino-*

_____4. eosinophils

_____5. agranulocyte

_____6. hemostasis

_____7. albumin

_____8. erythrocytes

_____9. glucose

_____10. platelets

_____11. plasma

_____12. hemoglobin

_____13. lymphocytes

_____14. *-phil*

_____15. whole blood

_____16. urea

_____17. monocytes

_____18. granulocyte

_____19. sodium

_____20. neutrophils

_____21. enucleated

_____22. macrophage

_____23. basophils

_____24. buffy coat

_____25. formed elements

A. is 91% water

B. an example of a waste product dissolved in plasma

C. cell fragments

D. an example of an electrolyte dissolved in plasma

E. having granules in the cytoplasm

F. increased numbers in allergies

G. produce antibodies

H. a protein that binds oxygen

I. a cell that is capable of engulfing another cell

J. an example of a plasma protein

K. transport oxygen and carbon dioxide

L. consists of leukocytes and platelets

M. a type of connective tissue

N. promote inflammation by releasing histamine

O. not having granules in the cytoplasm

P. a monocyte that has migrated into the tissue

Q. destroys bacteria by phagocytosis

R. a word part meaning rosy red

S. the process that stops bleeding

T. a nutrient dissolved in plasma

U. platelets are cytoplasmic fragments of this cell

V. term meaning "without a nucleus"

W. the cells and cell fragments of blood

X. a word part meaning attracted to

Y. the largest leukocyte

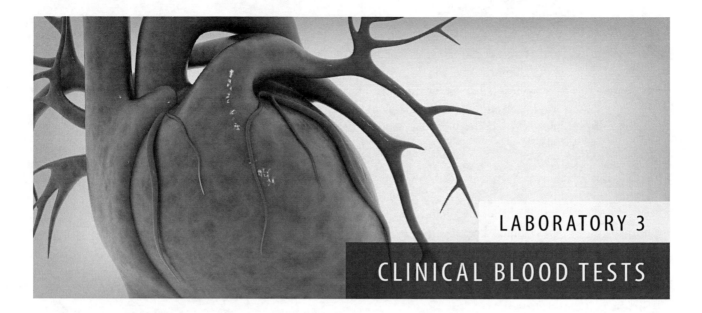

ANEMIA

Anemia is a group of conditions that result from the inability of erythrocytes to deliver the needed amount of oxygen to the cells of the body. There are two ways in which anemia can develop. The first is an insufficient number of erythrocytes and the second is the inability of the erythrocytes to bind the normal amount of oxygen (i.e. a problem with the hemoglobin).

Symptoms of anemia are all related to the insufficient supply of oxygen and include:

- fatigue – the muscles are not getting enough oxygen
- shortness of breath – feeling like you're not getting enough oxygen, but that is not the actual problem, it is a problem with not having enough RBCs or hemoglobin to carry oxygen from the lungs
- dizziness – the brain not getting enough oxygen
- numbness/tingling in hands and feet – these are at the end of the circulatory loop, therefore they are often the first tissues not to receive enough oxygen
- pale – the red color of blood gives light colored skin its pinkish color
- increased heart rate – heart is trying to pump more blood in order to get more oxygen to the body

This exercise will look at five different types of anemia: pernicious anemia, iron-deficiency anemia, aplastic anemia, sickle cell anemia, and hemorrhagic anemia.

Pernicious anemia:

Vitamin B_{12} is an essential vitamin. That means that it must be absorbed from the diet. It is a difficult vitamin to absorb because absorption requires intrinsic factor, a gastric enzyme. If the body fails to produce enough intrinsic factor, then a vitamin B_{12} deficiency develops, and the person is unable to properly make hemoglobin.

Iron-deficiency anemia:

Iron is the essential atom needed to synthesize normal hemoglobin. Iron is the part of the hemoglobin molecule that actually binds oxygen. Each molecule of hemoglobin contains four iron atoms. The body recycles iron from worn-out erythrocytes. Therefore, this condition develops in persons with an iron-poor diet or with bleeding problems whose diet does not replace the iron that is lost by bleeding. Two examples of conditions that may lead to iron-deficiency anemia are heavy menstrual periods and gastrointestinal bleeding.

Aplastic anemia:

This anemia is caused by the loss of blood-producing bone marrow tissue. It results in a reduction in the number of all types of blood cells. It may be caused by exposure to toxins, radiation or chemotherapy, autoimmune disorders, and viral infections.

Sickle cell anemia:

This is an inherited condition in which the body produces erythrocytes that take on a curved or sickle-shape under low oxygen conditions. Sickle-shaped RBCs are more fragile than normal erythrocytes and easily breaks as it speeds through the blood vessels. This is called a hemolytic (*hemo*– = blood and –*lytic* = destruction) anemia.

Hemorrhagic anemia:

This is anemia caused by the loss of blood volume. The blood loss may occur all at once from trauma to blood vessels or it may occur over a long period of time due to microscopic GI bleeding.

▶ For each type of anemia described, indicate its root cause: an insufficient number of RBCs or a problem with hemoglobin production.

    a.   pernicious

    b.   iron-deficiency anemia

    c.   aplastic

    d.   sickle

    e.   hemorrhagic

▶ Red blood cell count, hematocrit, and hemoglobin concentration can all diagnose different types of anemia. Explain how these three tests can diagnose anemia and help differentiate among different types of anemia.

Interpreting Blood Typing Results

▶ In each example below determine the blood type by studying the agglutination pattern and answering the antigen questions.

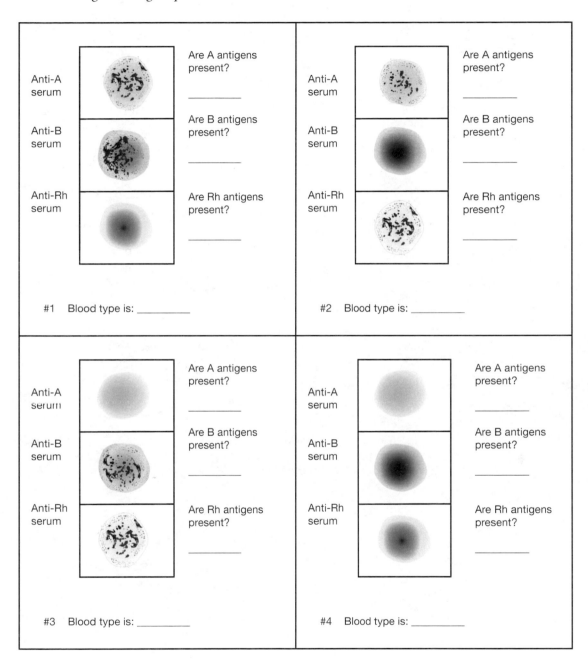

Anti-A serum
Are A antigens present?
_____

Anti-B serum
Are B antigens present?
_____

Anti-Rh serum
Are Rh antigens present?
_____

#1   Blood type is: _____

Anti-A serum
Are A antigens present?
_____

Anti-B serum
Are B antigens present?
_____

Anti-Rh serum
Are Rh antigens present?
_____

#2   Blood type is: _____

Anti-A serum
Are A antigens present?
_____

Anti-B serum
Are B antigens present?
_____

Anti-Rh serum
Are Rh antigens present?
_____

#3   Blood type is: _____

Anti-A serum
Are A antigens present?
_____

Anti-B serum
Are B antigens present?
_____

Anti-Rh serum
Are Rh antigens present?
_____

#4   Blood type is: _____

Key Term Matching

_____ 1. plasma

_____ 2. lymphocytes

_____ 3. hematocrit

_____ 4. hematopoiesis

_____ 5. pernicious anemia

_____ 6. megakaryocyte

_____ 7. agglutination

_____ 8. erythrocytes

_____ 9. antigen

_____ 10. leukocytes

_____ 11. hemocytometer

_____ 12. hemoglobinometer

_____ 13. hemoglobin

_____ 14. basophils

_____ 15. polycythemia vera

_____ 16. platelets

_____ 17. neutrophils

_____ 18. eosinophils

_____ 19. aplastic anemia

_____ 20. sicle cell anemia

A. transports oxygen and carbon dioxide

B. slide used to count RBCs

C. caused by vitamin B_{12} deficiency

D. WBCs

E. increased in persons with allergies

F. process that produces formed elements

G. molecule that stimulates antibody production

H. cell that fractures to produce platelets

I.   used to measure hemoglobin concentration

J.   increased by a viral infection

K. liquid matrix of blood

L. clumping of blood cells

M. condition of having too many RBCs

N. percentage of whole blood that is formed elements

O. iron-containing protein in RBCs

P. decreased by radiation exposure

Q. results from loss of blood-producing bone marrow

R. play a role in blood clotting process

S. an inherited condition

T. increased in parasitic infections

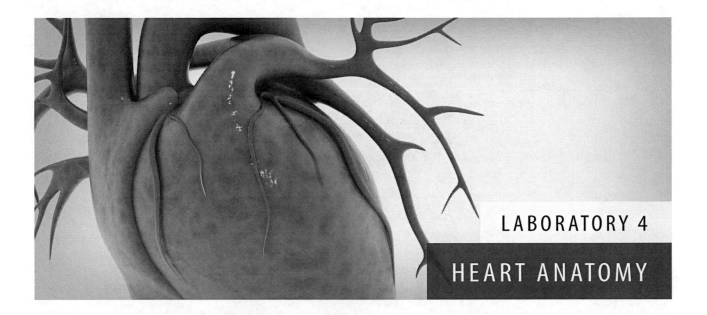

THROMBI, EMBOLI, AND INFARCTS

A **thrombus** is a blood clot that abnormally forms somewhere within the circulation. Because it extends into the open lumen of the blood vessel, the thrombus reduces blood flow downstream. This is called an **occlusion**. If a coronary artery becomes occluded, then the heart muscle served by that artery does not receive enough blood, a condition known as **ischemia**. The result is **angina pectoris**, the severe chest pain associated with coronary ischemia. If the coronary artery is completely blocked, then the heart muscle dies. This is a **myocardial infarction** (MI) or heart attack. The term **infarct** refers to the area of tissue that died from lack of oxygen. Another common site for thrombus formation is in the deep veins of the legs. This condition is called deep vein thrombosis (DVT). The symptoms of this condition include pain and redness at the site of the blood clot and swelling of the leg.

▶ Locate the anterior ventricular artery in Figure 4.1. Draw a thrombus in that artery and then shade in the area of the heart that would experience a myocardial infarction.

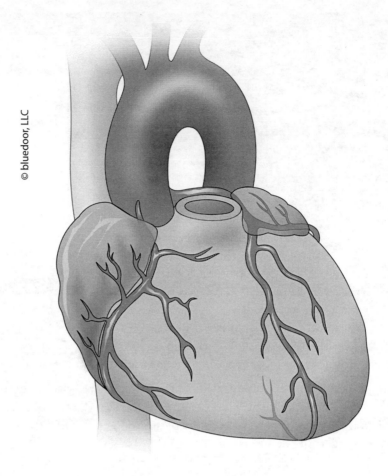

Figure 4.1: Myocardial infarct caused by occlusion of anterior ventricular artery.

However, there is another extremely dangerous (potentially fatal) result of having a thrombus, the formation of an **embolus**. An embolus occurs when a piece of the thrombus breaks off and moves through the circulation. As long as the embolus remains in the larger blood vessels there are no symptoms. But eventually the embolus reaches a vessel that is too small for it to fit through and it occludes (plugs) that vessel. This prevents blood from flowing to all the tissues downstream from the occlusion. If that tissue relies heavily on the blocked vessel for its oxygen then it may die, forming an infarct. The severity of this condition depends on the precise location of the occlusion, which downstream tissues are involved, and how large an area of tissue dies.

▶ Using an appropriate illustration from your textbook as a guide, list, in order, the flow of blood through both the pulmonary and systemic circuits. Begin with the right atrium and don't forget to include the heart valves.

If an embolus breaks off in a systemic vein in the leg:

It would be able to pass through:

It would occlude:

If an embolus formed in the left ventricle:

It would be able to pass through:

It would occlude:

Labeling Activity 1: External Heart Anatomy

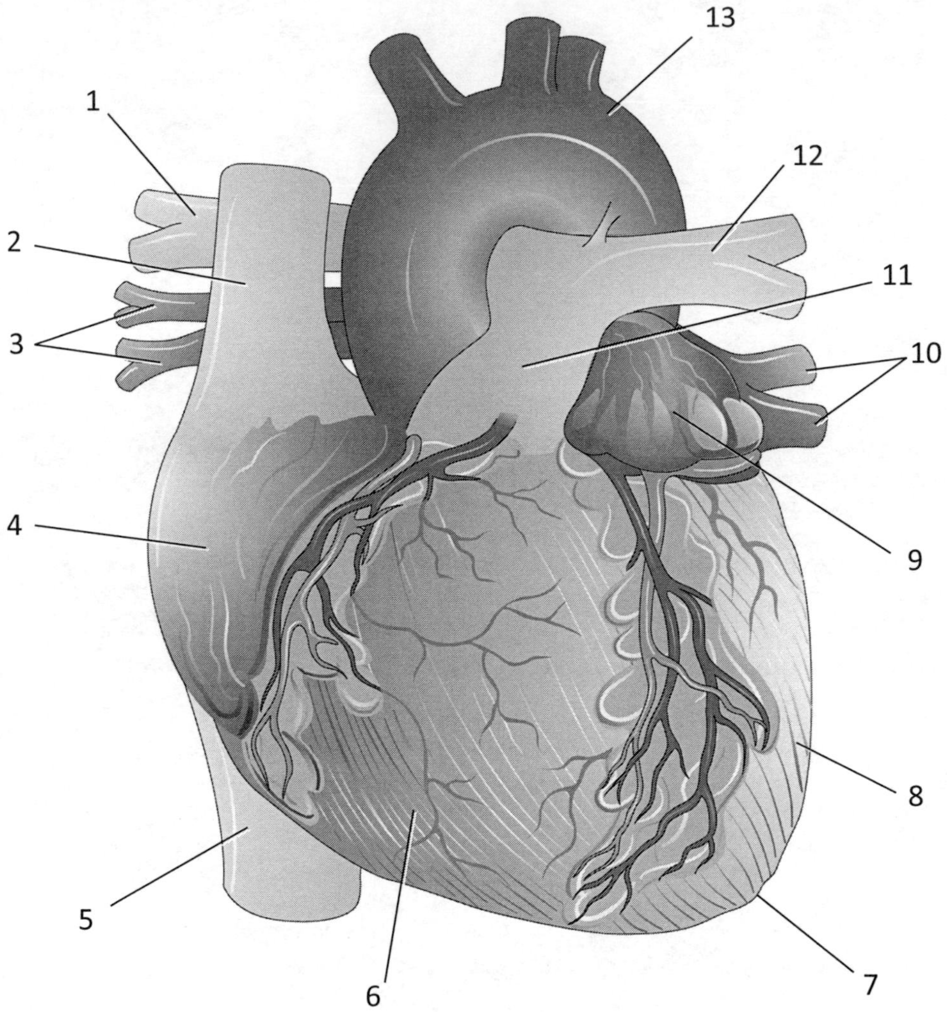

1. _____   8. _____

2. _____   9. _____

3. _____   10. _____

4. _____   11. _____

5. _____   12. _____

6. _____   13. _____

7. _____

Labeling Activity 2: Internal Heart Anatomy

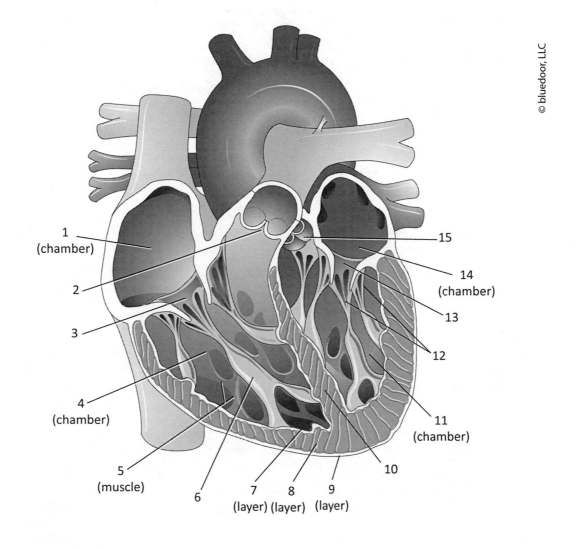

1
(chamber)

2

3

4
(chamber)

5
(muscle)

6

7
(layer)

8
(layer)

9
(layer)

10

11
(chamber)

12

13

14
(chamber)

15

1. _____

2. _____

3. _____

4. _____

5. _____

6. _____

7. _____

8. _____

9. _____

10. _____

11. _____

12. _____

13. _____

14. _____

15. _____

Key Term Matching

_____1. mediastinum

_____2. right atrium

_____3. marginal artery

_____4. aorta

_____5. trabeculae carneae

_____6. mitral valve

_____7. right ventricle

_____8. SA node

_____9. Purkinje fibers

_____10. base

_____11. endocardium

_____12. circumflex artery

_____13. inferior vena cava

_____14. aortic valve

_____15. left atrium

_____16. interventricular septum

_____17. pulmonary veins

_____18. cusp

_____19. visceral pericardium

_____20. apex

_____21. internodal pathway

_____22. papillary muscle

_____23. left ventricle

_____24. systemic capillary beds

_____25. pulmonary arteries

A. pumps blood into aorta

B. flap of a valve

C. broad superior region of heart

D. inner lining of heart

E. branch of right coronary artery

F. pumps blood into pulmonary trunk

G. deliver oxygen to tissues and organs

H. drains blood from lower body

I. contracts to tense chordae tendineae

J. location of the heart in thoracic cavity

K. separates left and right ventricles

L. stimulates atria to contract

M. largest artery in the body

N. epicardium

O. pacemaker of the heart

P. receives blood from superior vena cava

Q. stimulate ventricles to contract

R. carry deoxygenated blood to lungs

S. a semilunar valve

T. receives blood from pulmonary veins

U. also called bicuspid

V. ridges of cardiac muscle in ventricles

W. branch of left coronary artery

X. pointed tip of heart

Y. carry oxygenated blood from lungs

Coloring Activity 1: External Anatomy

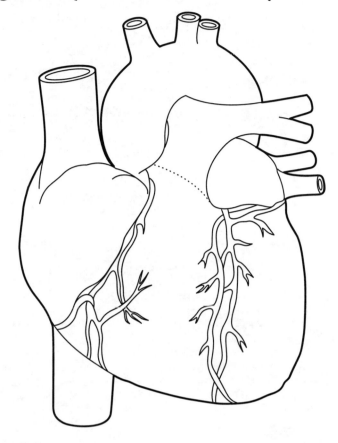

Aorta

Inferior vena cava

Left atrium

Left ventricle

Pulmonary arteries

Pulmonary trunk

Pulmonary veins

Right atrium

Right ventricle

Superior vena cava

Coloring Activity 2: Internal Features of the Heart

Color each of the terms differently, then match the color with the part corresponding to the number scheme.

AORTA **1**
PULMONARY TRUNK **2**
SUPERIOR VENA CAVA **3**
INFERIOR VENA CAVA **4**
INTERVENTRICULAR
SEPTUM **5**
MYOCARDIUM **6**
EPICARDIUM **7**
MITRAL VALVE **8**
TRICUSPID VALVE **9**
CHORDAE TENDINEAE **10**
PAPILLARY MUSCLE **11**
AORTIC SEMILUNAR
VALVE **12**
PULMONARY
SEMILUNAR VALVE **13**

RIGHT ATRIUM **14**
LEFT ATRIUM **15**
RIGHT VENTRICLE **16**
LEFT VENTRICLE **17**
PERICARDIUM **18**
FIBROUS LAYER OF
PARIETAL
PERICARDIUM **19**
SEROUS LAYER OF
PARIETAL
PERICARDIUM **20**
PERICARDIAL CAVITY **21**
ENDOCARDIUM **22**

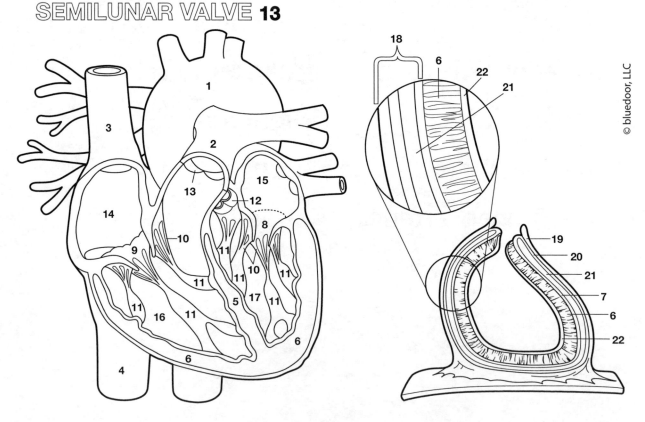

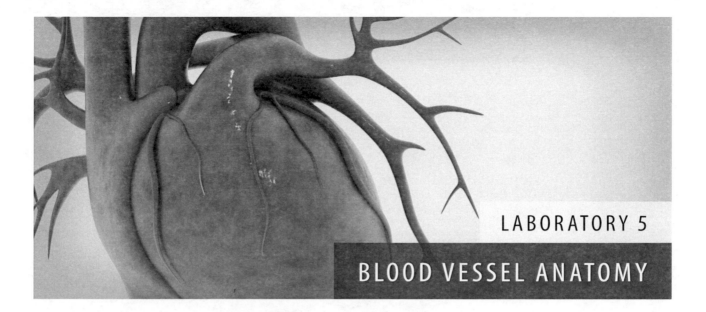

ATHEROSCLEROSIS

Cardiovascular disease (CVD) is a group of conditions affecting the heart and/or blood vessels. Two of the most common conditions in this group are myocardial infarctions (heart attacks) and cerebro-vascular accidents (strokes). According to the American Heart Association, 1 out of every 2.9 deaths in the United States is related to CVD, or 1 death every 38 seconds.

Atherosclerosis is one of the major causes of CVD. Atherosclerosis is the accumulation, over a long period of time, of cholesterol within the tunica interna of arteries. The presence of cholesterol begins a chain of events that may eventually produce a thrombus (blood clot) that occludes the artery causing the tissue it serves to die from lack of oxygen. Figure 5.1 describes the steps in this process.

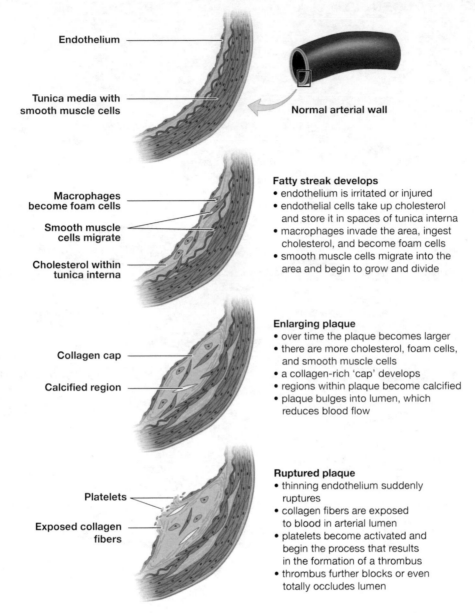

Endothelium

Tunica media with
smooth muscle cells

Normal arterial wall

Macrophages
become foam cells

Smooth muscle
cells migrate

Cholesterol within
tunica interna

Fatty streak develops
• endothelium is irritated or injured
• endothelial cells take up cholesterol
  and store it in spaces of tunica interna
• macrophages invade the area, ingest
  cholesterol, and become foam cells
• smooth muscle cells migrate into the
  area and begin to grow and divide

Collagen cap

Calcified region

Enlarging plaque
• over time the plaque becomes larger
• there are more cholesterol, foam cells,
  and smooth muscle cells
• a collagen-rich 'cap' develops
• regions within plaque become calcified
• plaque bulges into lumen, which
  reduces blood flow

Platelets

Exposed collagen
fibers

Ruptured plaque
• thinning endothelium suddenly
  ruptures
• collagen fibers are exposed
  to blood in arterial lumen
• platelets become activated and
  begin the process that results
  in the formation of a thrombus
• thrombus further blocks or even
  totally occludes lumen

Figure 5.1: The development and rupture of an atherosclerotic plaque.

There are multiple risk factors that increase the risk of developing CVD. Knowledge of these risk factors is important in helping individuals make healthy lifestyle choices. Some of these risk factors are uncontrollable, while others can be controlled or reduced. Below is a list of the risk factors known to be related to the development of CVD. For each risk factor, write whether it is controllable or uncontrollable. Then, for the controllable risk factors, write what a person could do to reduce their risk of developing CVD.

1. Family history of CVD

2. Sedentary lifestyle

3. Overweight

4. Age

5. Gender

6. Smoking

7. High blood pressure

Labeling Activity 1

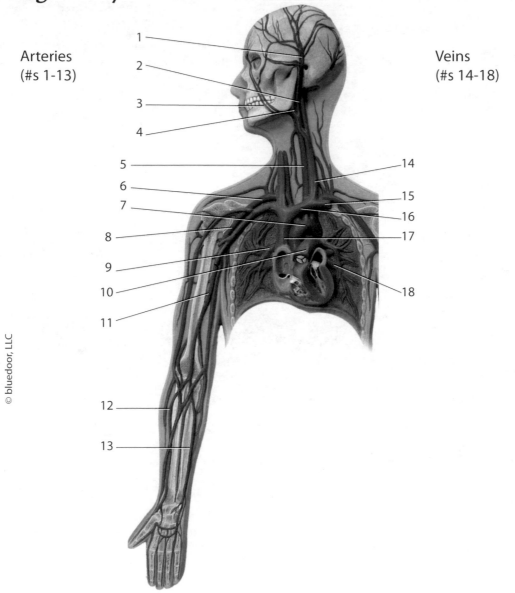

Arteries
(#s 1-13)

Veins
(#s 14-18)

© bluedoor, LLC

1. _____   10. _____

2. _____   11. _____

3. _____   12. _____

4. _____   13. _____

5. _____   14. _____

6. _____   15. _____

7. _____   16. _____

8. _____   17. _____

9. _____   18. _____

Labeling Activity 2

Arteries
(#s 1-10)

Veins
(#S 11-16)

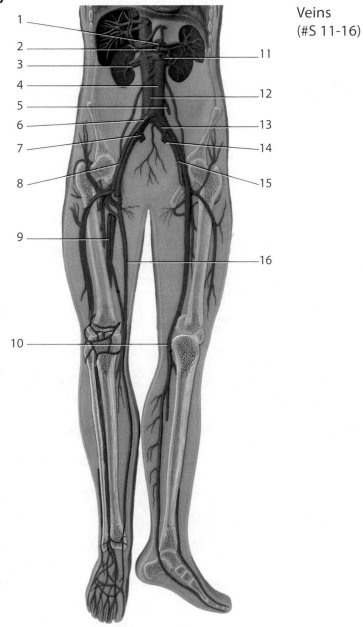

© bluedoor, LLC

1. _____   9. _____

2. _____   10. _____

3. _____   11. _____

4. _____   12. _____

5. _____   13. _____

6. _____   14. _____

7. _____   15. _____

8. _____   16. _____

Key Term Matching

_____ 1. endothelium

_____ 2. coronary arteries

_____ 3. common carotid artery

_____ 4. anterior cerebral artery

_____ 5. valves

_____ 6. arteries

_____ 7. celiac trunk

_____ 8. vertebral vein

_____ 9. radial artery

_____ 10. pulmonary arteries

_____ 11. thoracic aorta

_____ 12. renal vein

_____ 13. tunica externa

_____ 14. popliteal vein

_____ 15. internal elastic membrane

_____ 16. brachiocephalic artery

_____ 17. median sacral artery

_____ 18. external jugular vein

_____ 19. veins

_____ 20. pulmonary veins

_____ 21. inferior vena cava

_____ 22. capillaries

_____ 23. hepatic portal vein

_____ 24. tunica media

_____ 25. ulnar vein

A. a continuation of the aortic arch

B. a branch of the aortic arch

C. carry deoxygenated blood to lungs

D. carry blood toward the heart

E. drains blood from the head

F. carries blood to frontal and parietal lobes

G. composed of fibrous connective tissue

H. carries blood away from the kidneys

I. supply blood to myocardium

J. a branch of the abdominal aorta

K. drains blood from spinal cord and neck muscles

L. contains smooth muscle tissue

M. present in arteries but not veins

N. carries nutrients from digestive organs to liver

O. prevent backflow of blood

P. site of exchange between cells and bloodstream

Q. carry oxygenated blood to left atrium

R. carries blood to the head

S. carry blood away from the heart

T. an artery in the arm

U. composed of simple squamous epithelium

V. drains blood from abdomen and legs

W. drains blood from medial forearm

X. a vein in the leg

Y. supplies blood to the coccyx

Coloring Activity

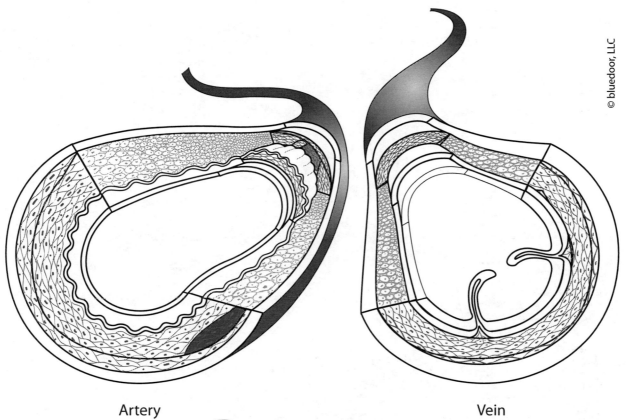

Artery   Vein

Basement membrane

Endothelium

Internal elastic membrane

Lumen

Tunica externa

Tunica media

Valve

Schematic Map of Systemic Arteries

▶ This is a schematic map of the systemic arteries. The arteries you are asked to identify have been numbered. Place the number for each systemic artery in the blank before its name.

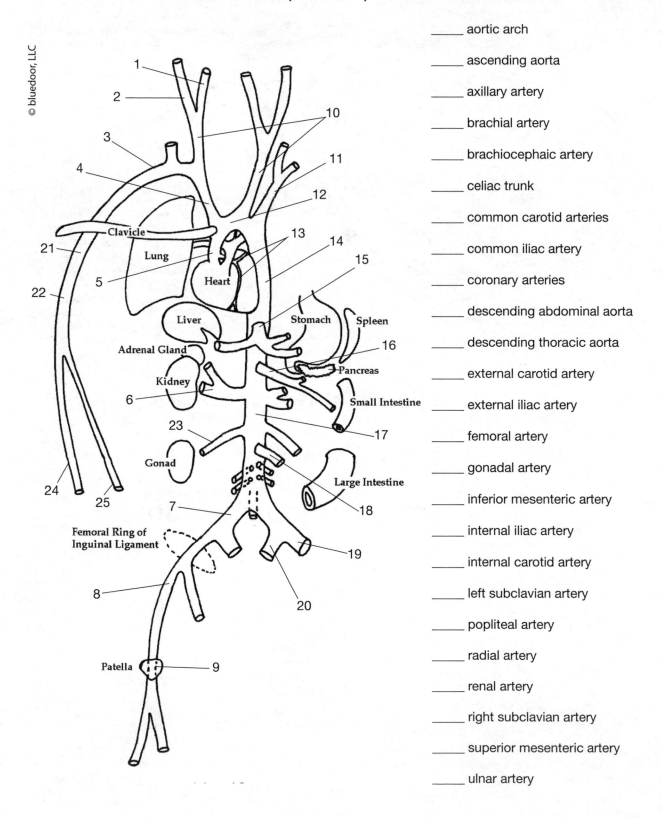

_____ aortic arch

_____ ascending aorta

_____ axillary artery

_____ brachial artery

_____ brachiocephaic artery

_____ celiac trunk

_____ common carotid arteries

_____ common iliac artery

_____ coronary arteries

_____ descending abdominal aorta

_____ descending thoracic aorta

_____ external carotid artery

_____ external iliac artery

_____ femoral artery

_____ gonadal artery

_____ inferior mesenteric artery

_____ internal iliac artery

_____ internal carotid artery

_____ left subclavian artery

_____ popliteal artery

_____ radial artery

_____ renal artery

_____ right subclavian artery

_____ superior mesenteric artery

_____ ulnar artery

Schematic Map of Systemic Veins

▶ This is a schematic map of the systemic veins. The veins you are asked to identify have been numbered. Place the number for each systemic vein in the blank before its name.

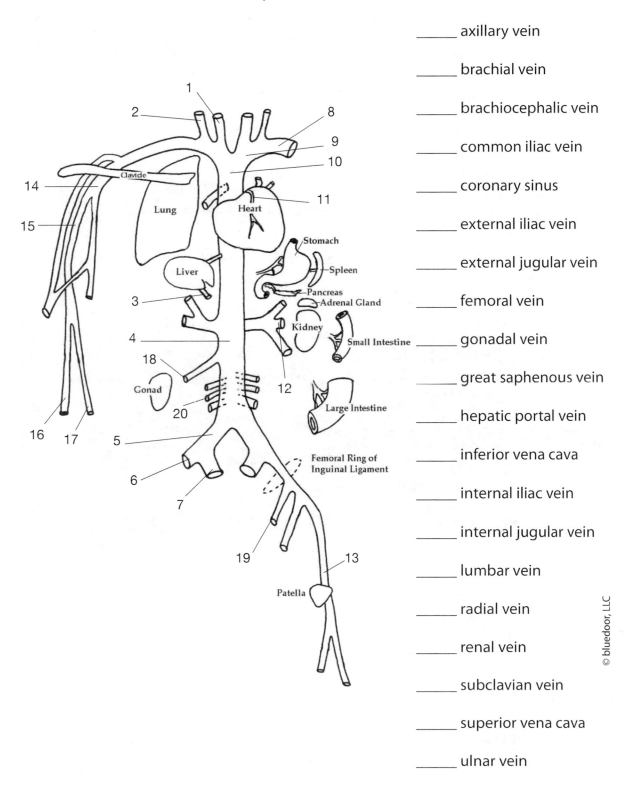

_____ axillary vein

_____ brachial vein

_____ brachiocephalic vein

_____ common iliac vein

_____ coronary sinus

_____ external iliac vein

_____ external jugular vein

_____ femoral vein

_____ gonadal vein

_____ great saphenous vein

_____ hepatic portal vein

_____ inferior vena cava

_____ internal iliac vein

_____ internal jugular vein

_____ lumbar vein

_____ radial vein

_____ renal vein

_____ subclavian vein

_____ superior vena cava

_____ ulnar vein

PULMONARY CIRCULATION

The pulmonary circulation begins as the right ventricle pushes blood into the pulmonary trunk during ventricular systole. From the pulmonary trunk, deoxygenated blood is carried to the right and left lungs by the right and left pulmonary arteries. Within the lungs, the exchange of respiratory gases occurs, resulting in a reduction of carbon dioxide and an increase of oxygen levels in the blood. The freshly oxygenated blood is carried to the left atrium by the pulmonary veins.

Exercise 5.1: Major vessels of the pulmonary circulation

You will study the major vessels of the pulmonary circulation in this observational exercise.

1. Using models and charts that are available in the lab, study the major vessels of the pulmonary circulation, which are listed below:

   pulmonary trunk   right pulmonary arteries
   left pulmonary arteries   right pulmonary veins
   left pulmonary veins

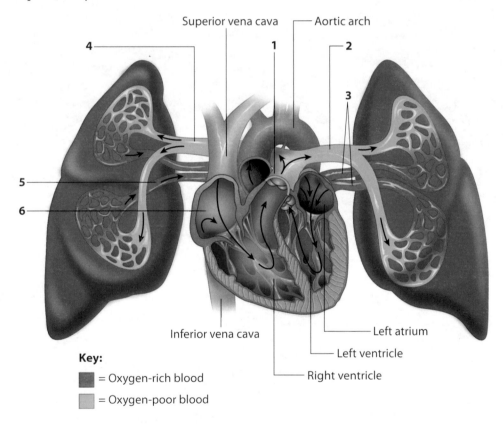

Figure 5.2: Pulmonary circulation.

Complete the labels in Figure 5.2. Record your answers in the spaces provided.

1. _____   4. _____

2. _____   5. _____

3. _____   6. _____

FETAL CIRCULATION

The fetal stage of life is characterized by a dependency on the mother for oxygen and nutrients and the removal of carbon dioxide and other wastes. The exchange between mother and fetus is made possible by the presence of a **placenta**, which contains capillaries from the mother. As blood flows through the maternal capillaries, oxygen and nutrients move into the placenta and are channeled into a single **umbilical vein**, which carries oxygen-rich blood through the umbilical cord to the fetus. Within the fetus, the **ductus venosus** carries blood from the umbilical vein to the inferior vena cava. In order to bypass circulation to the lungs, the **foramen ovale** permits blood to flow between the atria and the **ductus arteriosus** shunts blood from the pulmonary trunk into the aorta. To remove deoxygenated blood, two **umbilical arteries** channel it from their origin at the internal iliac arteries, through the umbilical cord, and to the placenta. At birth, the infant becomes independent of the mother quickly as the pulmonary circulation begins with the closure of the foramen ovale and constriction of the ductus arteriosus. Severing and tying the umbilical cord completes the circulatory changes, causing the umbilical vein, ductus venosus, and umbilical arteries to become unfunctional and they degenerate into vestigial structures.

Exercise 5.2: Fetal circulation

You will study the major vessels in fetal circulation and compare them to the changes that arise at birth in this exercise.

1. Using models and charts that may be available in the lab, review the fetal circulation and the changes that occur at birth. They are listed below:

    umbilical arteries   umbilical vein
    ductus venosus   foramen ovale
    ductus arteriosus

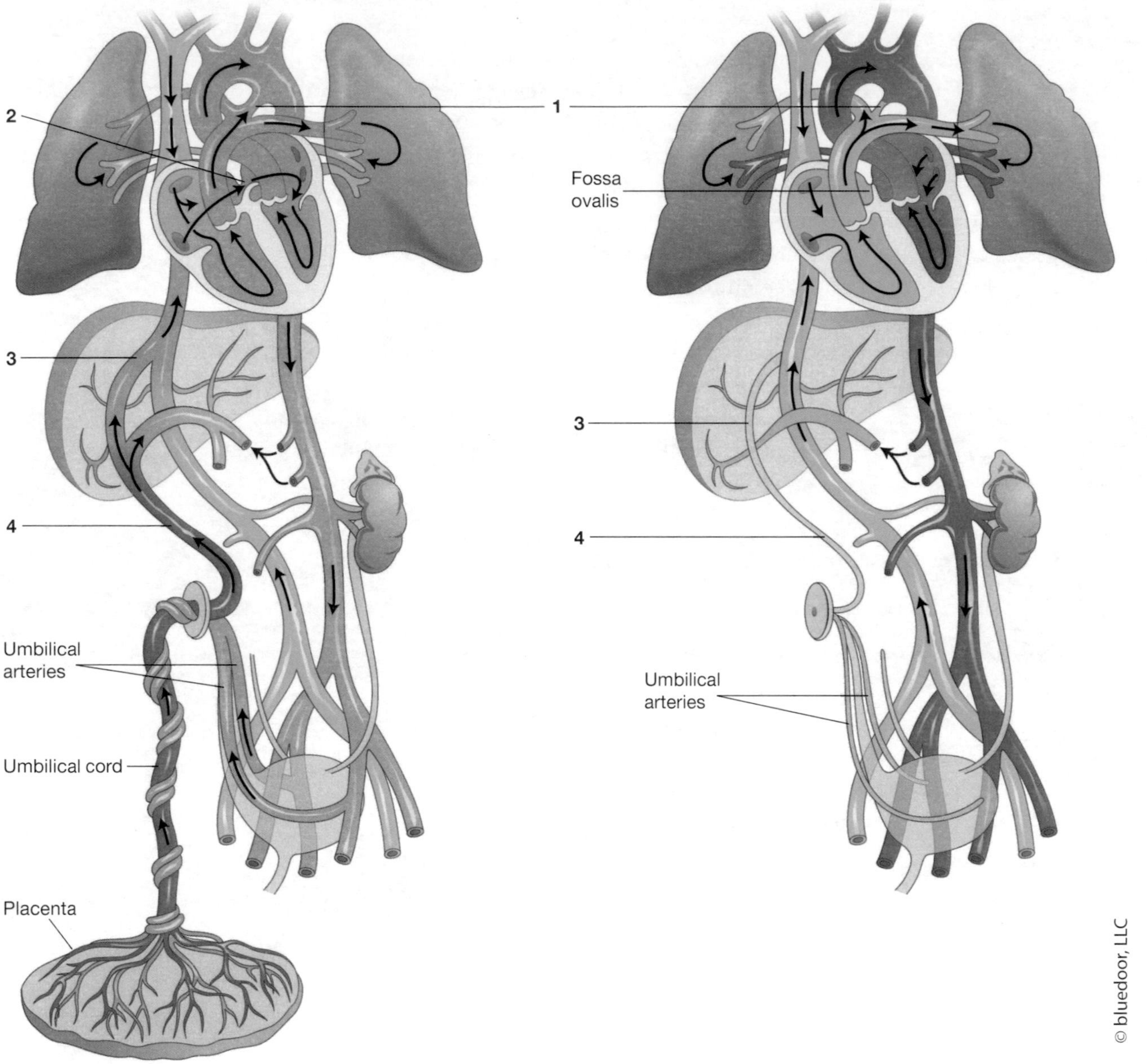

Figure 5.3: Fetal circulation. (a) Circulation of the fetus bypasses blood to the lungs and is dependent on exchange at the placenta. (b) Circulation of a newborn.

Complete the labels in Figure 5.3a and 5.3b. Record your answers in the spaces provided:

1. _____   3. _____

2. _____   4. _____

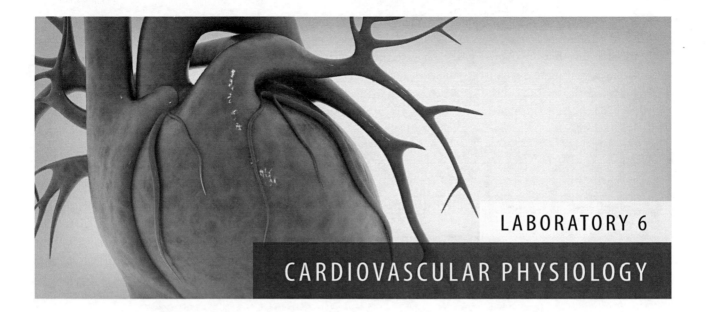

ARRHYTHMIAS

Arrhythmia is a general term that refers to a change in the rhythm of the heartbeat caused by a problem with the conduction system. The heart beats either too fast, too slow, or irregularly. If a person's heart rate is 80 bpm, then the heart beats 115,200 times each day. An occasional irregular heartbeat is normal and can be affected by everyday things, such as caffeine, nicotine, alcohol, stress, and physical activity. Arrhythmias may also be caused by medications, a hyperactive thyroid gland, and, most commonly, heart disease. Arrhythmias range from completely harmless to life threatening. The most dangerous arrhythmias reduce the heart's ability to pump blood effectively. Symptoms of these arrhythmias include shortness of breath, feeling light-headed, fatigue, dizziness, and fainting.

Many arrhythmias can be identified by electrocardiography (ECG or EKG). This procedure measures and records the wave of stimulation as it moves through the heart muscle via the conduction system. Heart muscle contracts when the stimulus is present and relaxes when the stimulus is not present. Therefore, the movement of the stimulus through the heart muscle reveals the pattern of contraction and relaxation.

Normal Sinus Rhythm

Normal sinus rhythm (NSR) is the characteristic rhythm of a healthy heart. The sinoatrial node is properly initiating the wave of stimulation and the wave properly spreads through the heart muscle. The ECG waves illustrated on the strip below have all the proper waves. The normal heart rate of a resting adult is between 60 and 100 bpm. The ECG strip below illustrates NSR.

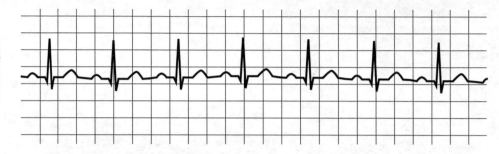

Examples of Arrhythmias

Bradycardia – The ECG wave is normal, but the heart rate is usually less than 60 bpm. This occurs when the SA node does not initiate the wave of stimulation often enough.

Ventricular tachycardia (V-tach) – The ECG shows multiple QRS complexes without visible P or T waves. This rhythm indicates damage to the ventricles.

Atrial flutter – Also called atrial fibrillation. The atria are being stimulated at a very fast rate. This results in a quivering of the atrial heart muscle. The ECG shows several small P waves before each QRS complex.

Ventricular fibrillation (V-fib) – There is no organized wave of stimulation spreading through the heart muscle. As a result, individual heart muscle cells contract independently leading to a quivering of the heart muscle. Since there is no coordinated contraction of the ventricles, blood is not effectively ejected from the heart. If V-fib continues, cardiac arrest follows.

▶ Identify the arrhythmia illustrated by each ECG strip below.

A.

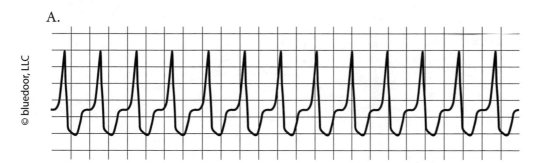

B.

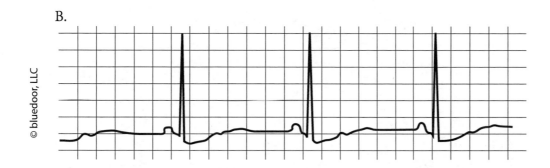

C.

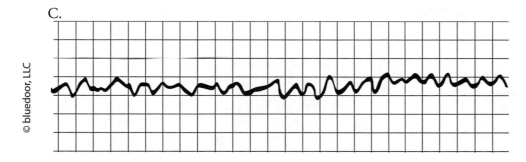

D.

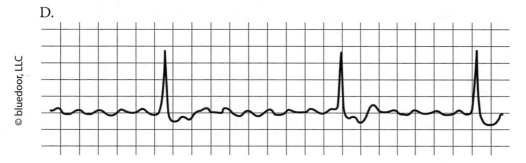

Labeling Activity

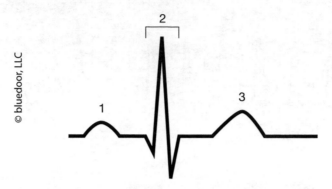

© bluedoor, LLC

1. a. Name the wave:

   b. Represents:

   c. What event follows this wave?

2. a. Name the wave:

   b. Represents:

   c. What event follows this wave?

3. a. Name the wave:

   b. Represents:

   c. What event follows this wave?

Key Term Matching

_____ 1. pulmonary valve

_____ 2. ventricular fibrillation

_____ 3. diastole

_____ 4. P wave

_____ 5. mitral valve

_____ 6. SA node

_____ 7. heartbeat

_____ 8. stethoscope

_____ 9. semilunar valves

_____10. systole

_____11. internodal pathway

_____12. aortic valve

_____13. bundle branches

_____14. cardiac cycle

_____15. QRS complex

_____16. AV valves

_____17. sphygmomanometer

_____18. tricuspid valve

_____19. NSR

_____20. lub

_____21. T wave

_____22. dup

_____23. bradycardia

_____24. auscultation

_____25. Purkinje fibers

A. represents atrial depolarization

B. contracting phase of cardiac cycle

C. heart muscle is quivering

D. heart valves found between an atrium and ventricle

E. distributes stimulus wave throughout atria

F. alternating contracting and relaxing of heart muscle

G. represents ventricular depolarization

H. the left semilunar valve

I. heart is beating too slowly

J. instrument used to listen to body sounds

K. the right atrioventricular valve

L. rhythm of a healthy heart

M. resting phase of cardiac cycle

N. represents ventricular repolarization

O. heart sound made when semilunar valves close

P. lasts for one cardiac cycle

Q. a network found in the ventricular walls

R. heart sound made when AV valves close

S. carry stimulus to the ventricles

T. the right semilunar valve

U. listening to

V. the pacemaker of the heart

W. heart valves between ventricles and great arteries

X. blood pressure cuff

Y. the left atrioventricular valve

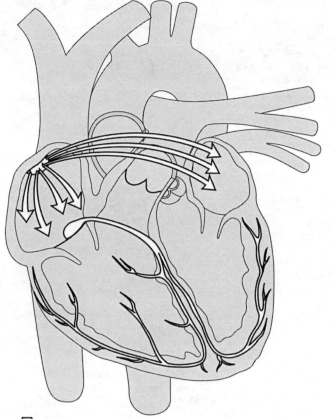

Atrioventricular bundle

Atrioventricular node

Internodal pathway

Left bundle branch

Purkinje fibers

Right bundle branch

Sinoatrial node

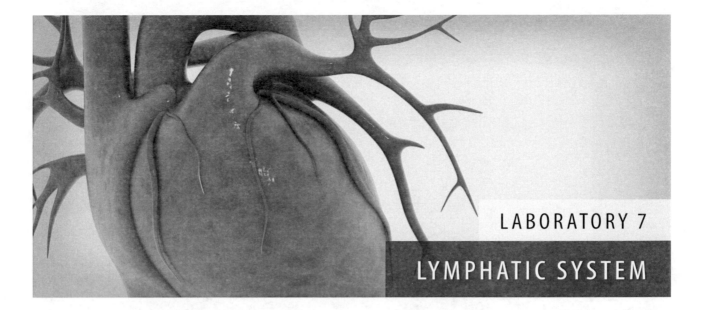

THE INFLAMMATORY RESPONSE

The **inflammatory response**, or inflammation, is a localized tissue reaction to injury. Tissue injury is caused by conditions such as:

- physical trauma such as that caused by blunt force, abrasions, or lacerations.
- exposure to toxic chemicals.
- exposure to extremes in temperature (either hot or cold).
- thermal, electrical, or chemical burns.
- infections by such pathogens as bacteria, viruses, and fungi.

Each of these examples either damages or kills cells, which begins a chain reaction.

1. In response, the damaged cells release chemicals into the interstitial fluid and produce cell debris.

2. The macrophages that live in the local area begin to remove cell debris and/or pathogens by **phagocytosis**. They also release chemical signals that attract more phagocytic cells into the area.

3. **Mast cells** are stimulated to release **histamine**.

4. Histamine targets the capillaries found at the site, causing them to dilate (**vasodilation**) and become more permeable. Vasodilation increases blood flow to the area which brings in more white blood cells and antibodies to fight infection and remove cell debris plus the proteins needed to repair the damage. Increased permeability allows these substances to move into the damaged tissue more easily.

5. The localized tissue changes caused by capillary vasodilation and increased permeability are responsible for producing the four hallmark signs of inflammation: **redness**, **swelling**, **heat**, and **pain**. The increased flow of red-colored blood into the area makes it appear redder (depending on your skin's natural color) and because this blood is warmer than the surrounding tissue, the area feels hot to the touch. Plasma leaks out of the capillaries, producing localized swelling. Pain is produced by both the impact of the injury on pain nerve endings and from pressure on

the pain nerves from the localized swelling.

6. As more white blood cells migrate into the area, the damage is eventually contained and removed. In the case of bacterial infections, pus is often produced. This is a combination of dead white blood cells, dead bacteria, cell debris, and tissue fluid produced during the height of fighting off a bacterial invasion.

7. After white blood cells remove all the debris and any pathogens that were introduced, tissue repair is able to proceed.

▶ This figure below illustrates an area of skin damaged by a nail. The steps of the inflammatory response are numbered. Below the figure is a summary of the inflammatory chain reaction, but they are out of order. Put them in order by placing the number before each step.

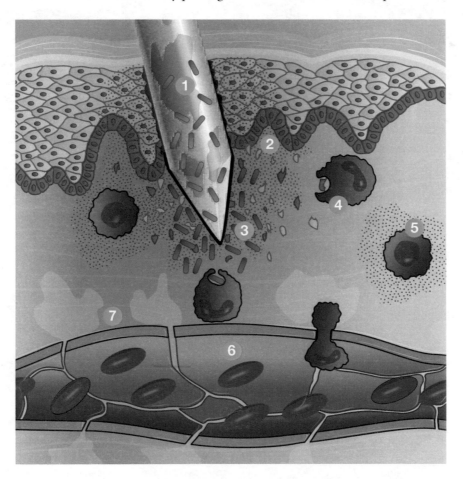

_____ Nail punctures through epidermis and into dermis.

_____ Plasma leaks out.

_____ Macrophages engulf bacteria and cell debris.

_____ Blood vessels dilate.

_____ Bacteria invade the wound.

_____ Damaged cells break apart, creating cell debris and releasing chemicals into interstitial space.

_____ Mast cells release histamine.

Labeling Activity

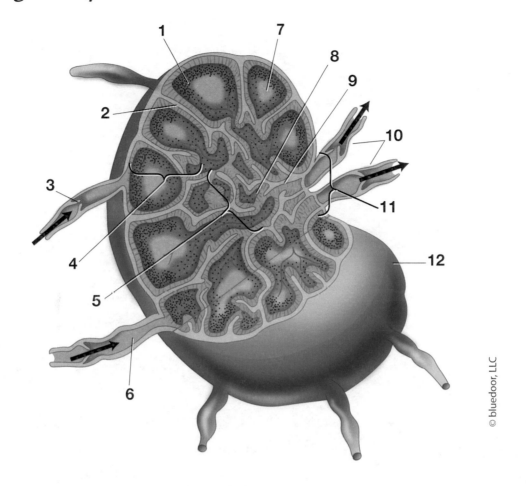

1. _____   7. _____

2. _____   8. _____

3. _____   9. _____

4. _____   10. _____

5. _____   11. _____

6. _____   12. _____

Key Term Matching

_____1. thymus gland   A. purify lymph from the arms

_____2. afferent lymphatic vessels   B. drains lymph from the thoracic cavity

_____3. lymphatic trunks   C. outer region of a lymph node

_____4. tonsils   D. largest lymphatic duct

_____5. valves   E. reservoir of blood

_____6. cortex   F. connective tissue cover of some lymphatic organs

_____7. axillary lymph nodes   G. receives lymph from right arm and upper body

_____8. trabeculae   H. contains venous sinuses in spleen

_____9. bronchomediastinal trunk   I. purify lymph from the legs

_____10. thoracic duct   J. hallmarks of inflammation

_____11. Hassall's corpuscle   K. receives lymph from intestinal trunk

_____12. capsule   L. process of shrinking and becoming fibrous

_____13. inguinal lymph nodes   M. site of T-cell maturation

_____14. heat, swelling, pain, redness   N. distinguishing feature of the thymus gland

_____15. MALT   O. carry lymph into lymph nodes

_____16. efferent lymphatic vessels   P. delivers lymph to lymphatic ducts

_____17. cervical lymph nodes   Q. location of the thymus gland

_____18. white pulp   R. located in the pharynx

_____19. medulla   S. central core of a lymph node

_____20. spleen   T. prevent backflow of lymph

_____21. mediastinum   U. fibrous extensions of a capsule

_____22. right lymphatic duct   V. example is lymphatic nodules in digestive tract wall

_____23. involution   W. carry lymph away from lymph nodes

_____24. cysterna chyli   X. purify lymph from the head

_____25. red pulp   Y. also called a splenic nodule

Coloring Activity

▶ In this coloring exercise, you will need to choose a color for each region of lymph nodes and then draw your own lymph nodes on the figure.

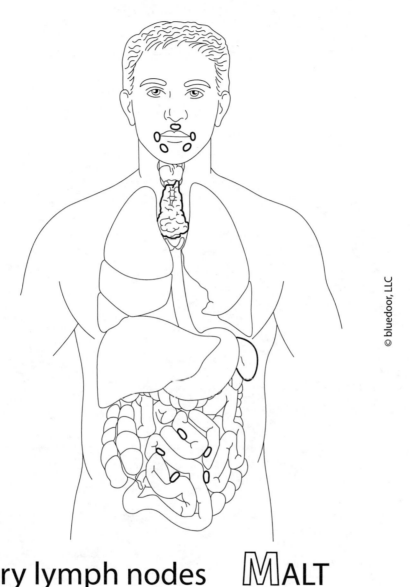

© bluedoor, LLC

Axillary lymph nodes   **M**ALT

Cervical lymph nodes   **S**pleen

Inguinal lymph nodes   **T**onsils

Thymus gland

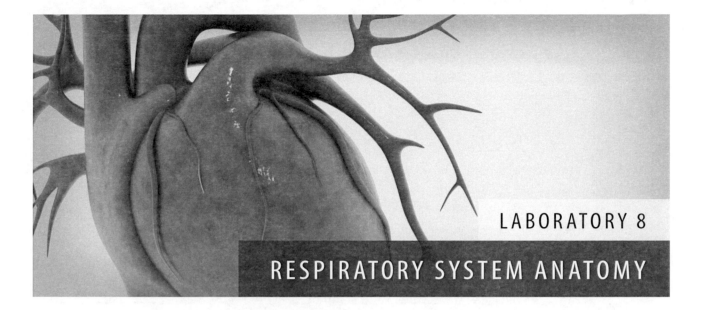

RESPIRATORY SYSTEM ANATOMY

CHRONIC OBSTRUCTIVE PULMONARY DISEASE

Chronic obstructive pulmonary disease (COPD) affects about 30 million Americans and is the-fourth-leading cause of death following heart disease, cancer, and cerebrovascular disease. Looking closely at the name, COPD, gives a general idea regarding what is causing the symptoms of this condition. *Chronic* indicates that the condition is of a long-standing and recurrent nature. The term *obstructive* describes conditions in which there is a blockage or obstruction to the free flow of air. A person with an obstructive condition has to expend more energy to move the same volume of air as does a person with healthy lungs. *Pulmonary disease* tells us that the problem is in the lungs.

Although there is some slight genetic predisposition to developing COPD, by far and away the primary cause of this condition is exposure to toxic substances, and the most common toxic substance is cigarette smoke. Both smokers and those exposed to secondhand smoke are at higher risk for developing COPD. Other sources of toxic substances include air pollution and occupational exposure to dust, gases, and chemical vapors. Men are twice as likely to have COPD because older men were more likely to smoke their whole lives than older women. The incidence of COPD in women is increasing as a greater percentage of women smoke. COPD is a general term for a group of specific conditions, each one having a different location and type of lung damage. The two most common are **emphysema** and **chronic bronchitis.**

Emphysema

Emphysema is a condition affecting the alveoli. Alveoli are arranged in clusters at the end of a respiratory bronchiole (think of a bunch of grapes). With repeated and long-term exposure to smoke, the structure of the alveoli accumulate damage, each alveolus becomes enlarged, and the walls between adjacent alveoli break down, causing them to merge into large air sacs. The end result is that instead of having a large "cluster of grapes," there is a much smaller number of "overinflated balloons." The name emphysema comes from a Greek word meaning *to inflate* or *distend*. At first glance, the problem with the balloon arrangement may not be apparent. After all, balloons hold a large volume of air. The problem is that with the loss of alveolar walls, there is also a loss of surface area for the respiratory membrane. This membrane, formed from the alveolar wall and the pulmonary capillaries, is the site of gas exchange. Any condition that reduces the area of the respiratory membrane impairs a person's ability to exchange oxygen for carbon dioxide. As a result, the major symptom of emphysema is shortness of breath with any mild exercise.

Chronic Bronchitis

Chronic bronchitis, as the name implies, is a condition affecting the bronchi. These airways are lined with pseudostratified ciliated columnar epithelium (PCCE) with goblet cells. Goblet cells secrete sticky mucus, which traps particles and pathogens to prevent them from reaching the alveoli. Then the cilia, which beat in a coordinated pattern, sweep the mucus up and out of the bronchial tree. In response to irritation, PCCE develops more goblet cells, which leads to more mucus, producing a thick coating on the inner walls of the bronchi. There are three problems with this thick layer of mucus. First, it reduces the diameter of the lumen, obstructing easy air flow. Second, the cilia are not able to effectively move the thick layer of mucus up and out of the airways. And third, this layer of mucus is a good breeding ground for pathogens that become lodged in it. This leads to the symptoms of chronic bronchitis: a chronic productive cough (sputum is raised), shortness of breath, wheezing, and repeated infections for at least three months of the year.

▶ The next figure is an illustration of normal clusters of alveoli. Next to this figure, make a sketch that illustrates the changes in alveoli caused by emphysema.

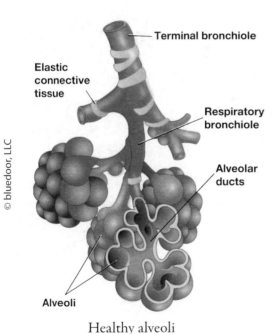

© bluedoor, LLC

Healthy alveoli   Alveoli with emphysema

▶ The photomicrographs below illustrate PCCE in the airways of a healthy person and a person with chronic bronchitis. Describe the differences you see in the two figures.

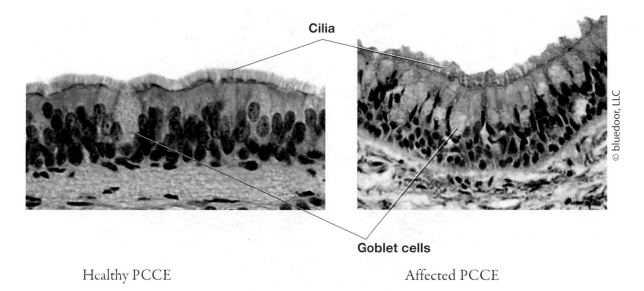

Cilia

Goblet cells

Healthy PCCE   Affected PCCE

© bluedoor, LLC

Labeling Activity 1

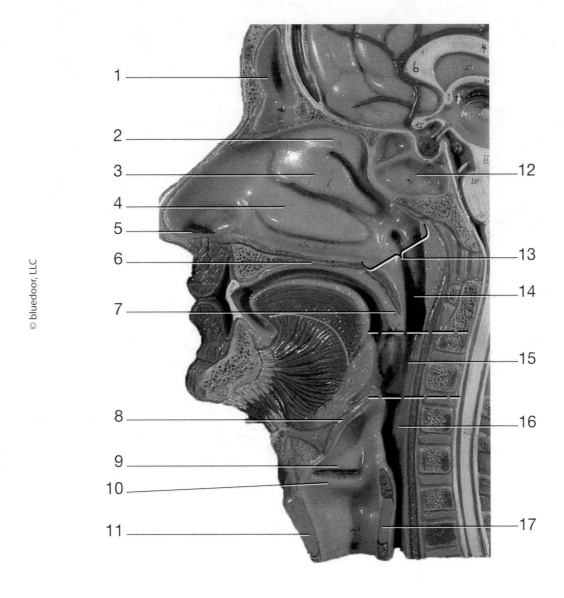

1. _____
2. _____
3. _____
4. _____
5. _____
6. _____
7. _____
8. _____
9. _____
10. _____
11. _____
12. _____
13. _____
14. _____
15. _____
16. _____
17. _____

© bluedoor, LLC

Labeling Activity 2

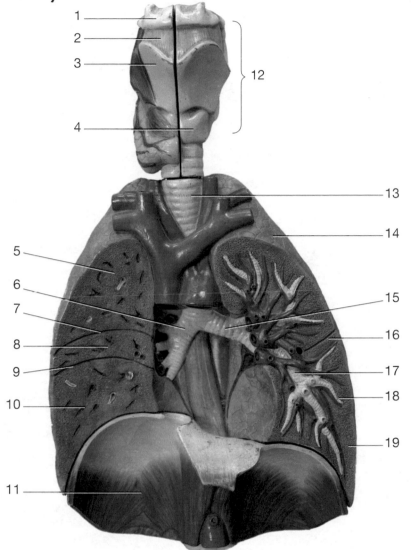

1. _____   11. _____

2. _____   12. _____

3. _____   13. _____

4. _____   14. _____

5. _____   15. _____

6. _____   16. _____

7. _____   17. _____

8. _____   18. _____

9. _____   19. _____

10. _____

Key Term Matching

_____1. lower respiratory tract   A. portion of pharynx receiving air from nasal cavity

_____2. vestibular folds   B. also known as lobar bronchi

_____3. oropharynx   C. consists of nose, pharynx, and larynx

_____4. vestibule   D. also known as the windpipe

_____5. secondary bronchi   E. shelf-like structures in nasal cavity

_____6. thyroid cartilage   F. forms most of posterior wall of larynx

_____7. nasal conchae   G. site of gas exchange

_____8. terminal bronchioles   H. divides the nasal cavity vertically

_____9. goblet cells   I. covers opening of trachea during swallowing

_____10. alveoli   J. formed by branching of bronchioles

_____11. upper respiratory tract   K. located in nasopharynx

_____12. trachea   L. a serous membrane linig the pleural cavity

_____13. nasopharynx   M. forms the anterior wall of the larynx

_____14. epiglottis   N. consists of trachea and bronchial tree

_____15. tertiary bronchi   O. point at which primary bronchi arise

_____16. nasal septum   P. secrete mucus

_____17. carina   Q. also known as segmental bronchi

_____18. pharyngeal tonsil   R. entry chamber of the nasal cavity

_____19. hilus   S. also known as the voice box

_____20. cricoid cartilage   T. false vocal cords

_____21. hard palate   U. opening between nasal cavity and nasopharynx

_____22. vocal folds   V. area of lung where bronchi and blood vessels enter

_____23. larynx   W. extends from soft palate to base of tongue

_____24. internal nares   X. true vocal cords

_____25. pleura   Y. forms part of the floor of nasal cavity

Coloring Activity

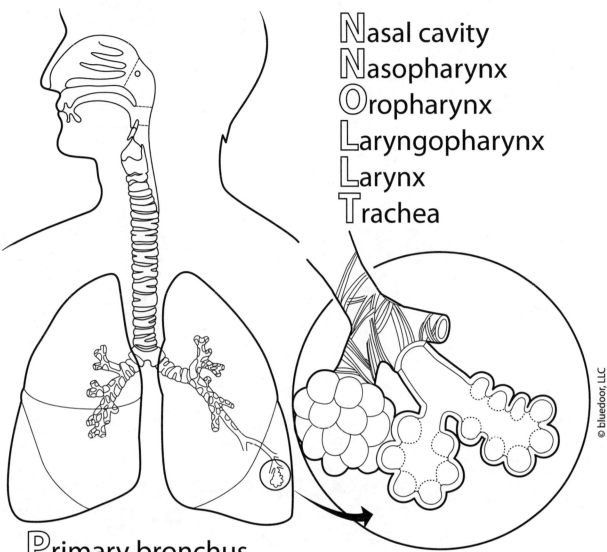

Nasal cavity
Nasopharynx
Oropharynx
Laryngopharynx
Larynx
Trachea

© bluedoor, LLC

Primary bronchus
Secondary bronchus
Tertiary bronchus
Bronchiole
Right superior lobe
Right middle lobe
Right inferior lobe

Terminal bronchiole
Respiratory bronchiole
Alveolar duct
Alveolus
Left superior lobe
Left inferior lobe

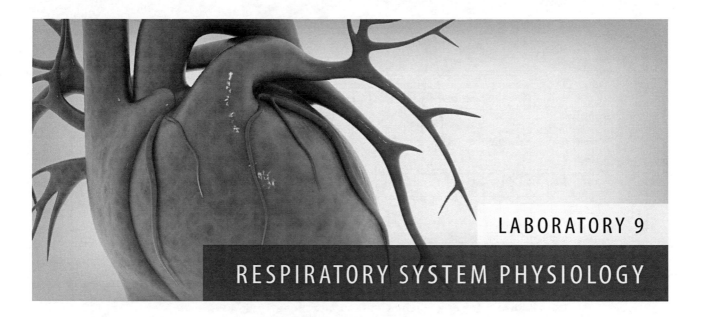

LUNG VOLUMES AND CAPACITIES

People do not move the same volume of air with each breath. Quiet or normal breathing moves approximately 500 mL of air. Beyond the amount of air moved during quiet breathing, people are capable of deep inhalations and forceful exhalations, each moving more air. These variations in the volume of air are called the respiratory volumes and respiratory capacities. These are defined in Table 9.1 and illustrated in Figure 9.1.

Table 9.1: Definition and average values for lung volumes and capacities for an adult.

VOLUME OR CAPACITY	DEFINITION	AVERAGE VALUE FOR A HEALTHY ADULT (mL)	
		Male	Female
Tidal Volume (V_T)	Volume of air moving into or out of lungs during quiet breathing	500	500
Inspiratory Reserve Volume (IRV)	Maximum volume of air that can be inhaled above tidal volume	3,300	1,900
Expiratory Reserve Volume (ERV)	Maximum volume of air that can be exhaled below tidal volume	1,000	700
Residual Volume (RV)	Volume of air that remains in respiratory system after a maximal exhalation	1,200	1,100
Inspiratory Capacity (IC)	V_T + IRV	3,800	2,400
Functional Residual Capacity (FRC)	ERV + RV	2,200	1,800
Vital Capacity (VC)	IRV + V_T + ERV	4,800	3,100
Total Lung Capacity (TLC)	IRV + V_T + ERV + RV	6,000	4,200

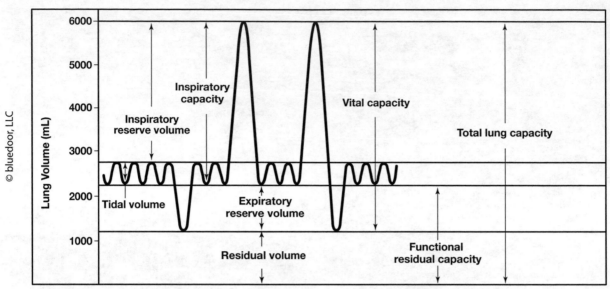

Figure 9.1: Lung volumes and capacities for average adult male.

Labeling Activity

▶ Below are graphs similar to Figure 9.1. Using the average values presented in Table 9.1, draw the four respiratory volumes on the upper graph and the four respiratory capacities on the lower graph.

The Respiratory Volumes

The Respiratory Capacities

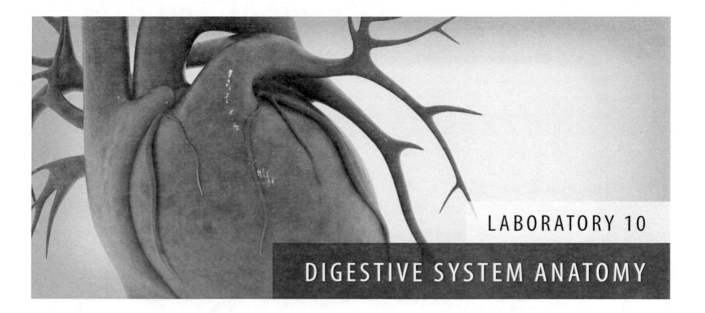

COLON PATHOLOGIES

Diverticulosis – **Diverticula** are pouch-like sacs that sometimes form along the colon. They protrude through the muscularis externa and appear as bumps on the outside of the colon. By themselves, diverticula are not dangerous. However, if stool or undigested food becomes trapped in a diverticulum, then **diverticulitis** develops. Symptoms may include pain and fever. An inflamed divertuculum may even rupture.

Bacterial colitis – The colon is full of helpful bacteria. They produce vitamins that the colon then absorbs. They also hold down the growth of harmful bacteria by out-competing them for resources. Occasionally, when antibiotics are overused, the helpful bacteria are killed. This allows pathological bacteria to grow unchecked, leading to bacterial colitis. One symptom of some bacterial infections is pus. This yellowish, semi-solid fluid is a combination of cell debris, dead bacteria, dead white blood cells, and tissue fluid.

Polyposis – **Polyps** are small growths that protrude out from the wall of the GI tract into the lumen. Some grow with a stalk, giving them a mushroom-like appearance. Polyps may be benign or precancerous. Polyps rarely cause any symptoms unless they are becoming cancerous. They are typically discovered and removed during a colonoscopy.

Colon cancer – Cancerous tumors develop in the lining of the colon or rectum. As a tumor grows larger, it begins to grow into the wall of the colon and invades surrounding tissues. It can then metastasize to regional lymph nodes and liver. There are few early symptoms. The tumor may bleed so slowly that the blood is not noticed in the stool. A large tumor may cause a blockage of the lumen, preventing food from moving through the colon.

Ulcerative colitis – Chronic condition in which colon becomes inflamed and develops multiple small ulcers, which appear red and raw. The exact cause of this condition is not well understood. Symptoms include abdominal cramping and bloody diarrhea.

Adhesions — Adhesions are scar tissue that develops as a result of previous surgery, infection, or inflammation. Scar tissue may form tight bands around the colon that restrict movement of material through the colon and may result in a total blockage.

Appendicitis — This is the sudden inflammation of the appendix. The appendix is hollow, making a blockage of the appendix the start of appendicitis. As a result, it becomes extremely inflamed and infected and may rupture. A rupture releases bacteria-filled intestinal contents into the abdominal cavity and leads to potentially life-threatening infections.

Crohn's disease (regional enteritis) — This is a chronic inflammation of the intestinal lining. It may affect any part of the GI tract, but most commonly occurs in the last portion of the ileum, just before it connects to the cecum. Symptoms include chronic diarrhea, abdominal cramps, fever, appetite loss, and weight loss. Crohn's disease is possibly an autoimmune disease.

▶ The figure below illustrates the colon pathologies described above. Using the figure and descriptions as clues, identify each pathology.

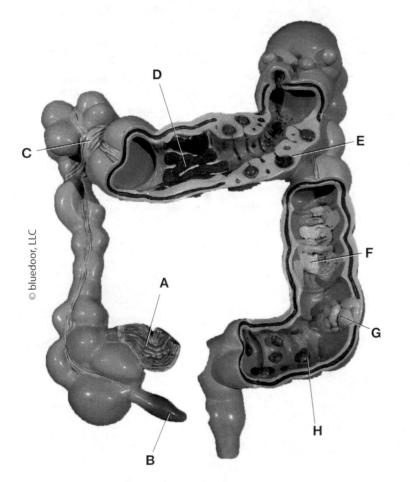

A. _____

B. _____

C. _____

D. _____

E. _____

F. _____

G. _____

H. _____

Labeling Activity 1

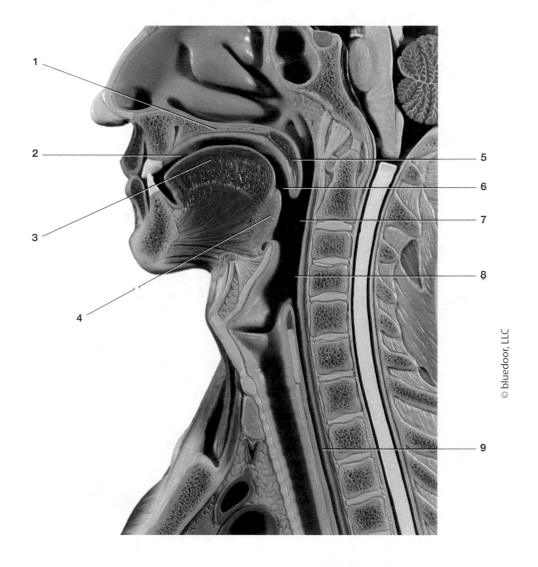

© bluedoor, LLC

1. _____   6. _____
2. _____   7. _____
3. _____   8. _____
4. _____   9. _____
5. _____

Labeling Activity 2

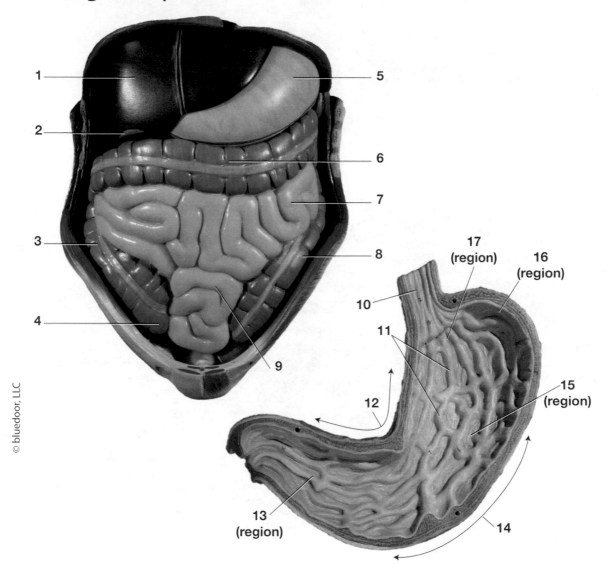

1. _____   10. _____

2. _____   11. _____

3. _____   12. _____

4. _____   13. _____

5. _____   14. _____

6. _____   15. _____

7. _____   16. _____

8. _____   17. _____

9. _____

Labeling Activity 3

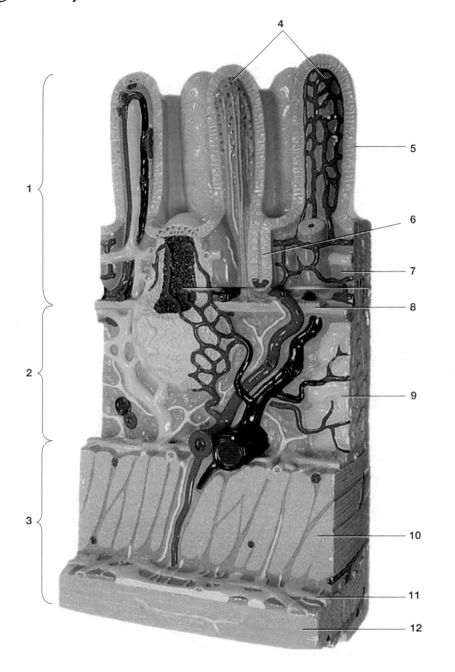

1. _____   7. _____
2. _____   8. _____
3. _____   9. _____
4. _____   19. _____
5. _____   11. _____
6. _____   12. _____

Key Term Matching

_____1. accessory organs

_____2. fundus

_____3. uvula

_____4. villi

_____5. large intestine

_____6. root

_____7. dentin

_____8. lamina propria

_____9. fauces

_____10. chyme

_____11. incisor

_____12. parietal cells

_____13. crown

_____14. stomach

_____15. cheeks

_____16. serosa

_____17. enamel

_____18. stratified squamous

_____19. gingivae

_____20. small intestine

_____21. pharynx

_____22. liver

_____23. molar

_____24. mucins

_____25. acinar cells

A. forms bulk of tooth

B. performs compaction

C. a cutting tooth

D. liquid food mixture in stomach

E. posterior opening of oral cavity

F. has three muscularis externa layers

G. portion of tooth above gum line

H. epithelium found in esophagus

I. are connected to GI tract by a duct

J. composed of loose connective tissue

K. dome-shaped stomach region

L. substance harder than bone

M. organ shared with respiratory system

N. exocrine part of pancreas

O. projection off of soft palate

P. in saliva to lubricate food

Q. finger-like extensions of mucosa

R. portion of tooth below gum line

S. the gums

T. performs 90% of digestion and absorption

U. secretes bile

V. a grinding tooth

W. secrete HCl

X. outermost layer of GI tract wall

Y. lateral walls of the oral cavity

Coloring Activity 1

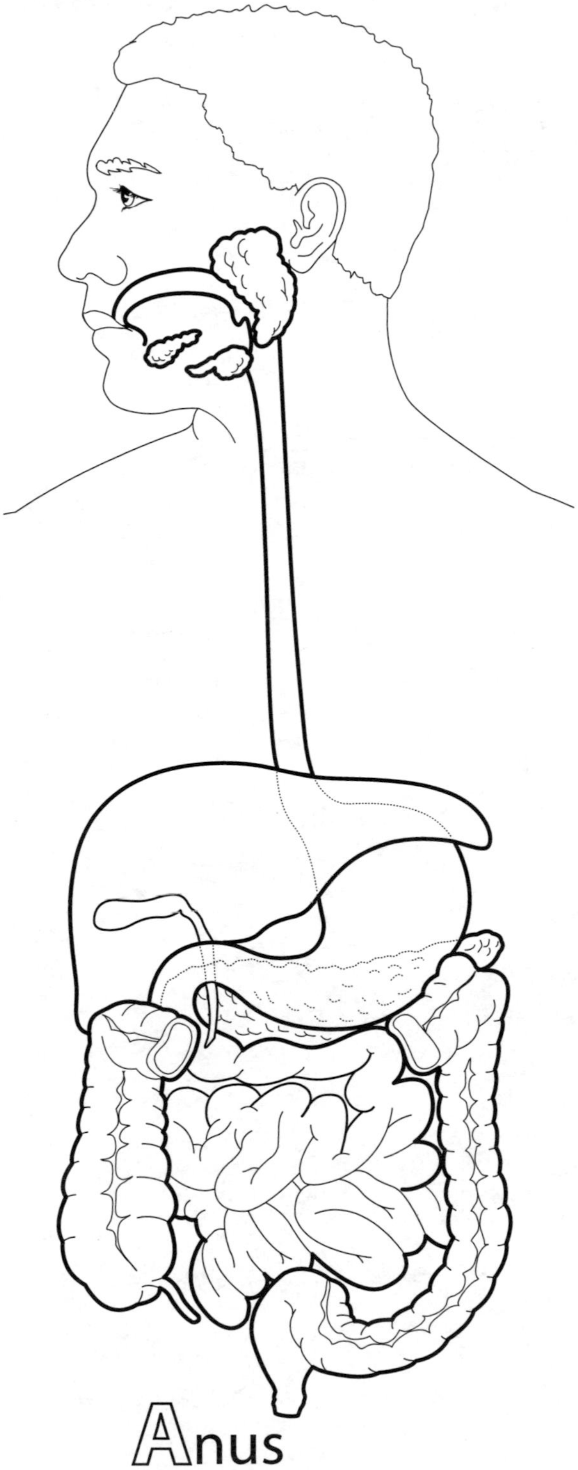

Cecum
Common bile duct
Descending colon
Duodenum
Esophagus
Gallbladder
Jejunum and ileum
Liver
Oral cavity
Pancreas
Parotid gland
Pharynx
Rectum
Sigmoid colon
Stomach
Sublingual gland
Submandibular gland
Tongue
Transverse colon

Anus
Appendix
Ascending colon

Coloring Activity 2

Coloring activity of GI tract wall structure. Color each of the terms differently, then match the color with the part corresponding to the number scheme.

VISCERAL PERITONEUM **1**
CONNECTIVE TISSUE
OF SEROSA **2**

Muscularis
LONGITUDINAL LAYER **3**
CIRCULAR LAYER **4**

Submucosa
SUBMUCOSA **5**

Mucosa
LAMINA PROPRIA **6**

LINING EPITHELIUM **7**

SUBMUCOSAL GLAND **8**
SUBMUCOSAL
PLEXUS **9**
NERVE **10**
BLOOD VESSEL **11**
FOLD OF PARIETAL
PERITONEUM **12**
ACCESSORY GLAND
OUTSIDE OF TRACT **13**

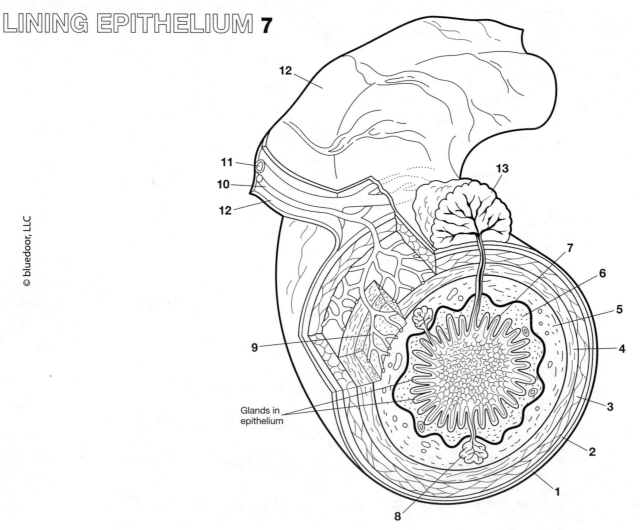

Glands in
epithelium

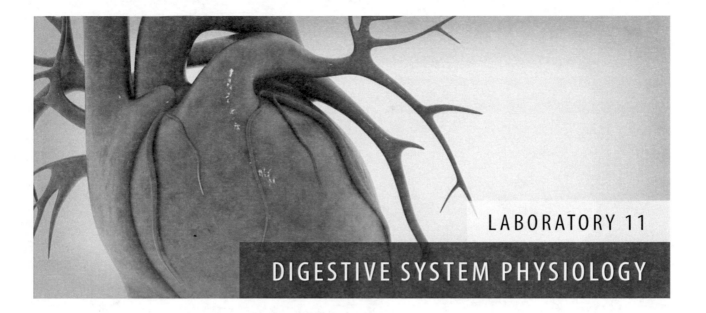

DIGESTIVE SYSTEM PHYSIOLOGY

CARBOHYDRATE DIGESTION

The primary dietary source of carbohydrates is **starch**, a large **glucose** polymer, found in bread, pasta, and potatoes. Starch digestion begins in the mouth through the action of salivary **amylase**, an enzyme produced by the salivary glands and added to the mouth in saliva. Amylase breaks down starch into **maltose**, a glucose disaccharide. The process is completed in the small intestine with additional amylase from the pancreas. Two disaccharides, **lactose** (milk sugar) and **sucrose** (table sugar) are also dietary sources of carbohydrates. These molecules, along with maltose, are broken down in the small intestine into three monosaccharides, glucose, **galactose**, and **fructose**. These monosaccharide molecules are then absorbed into the bloodstream across the GI tract wall.

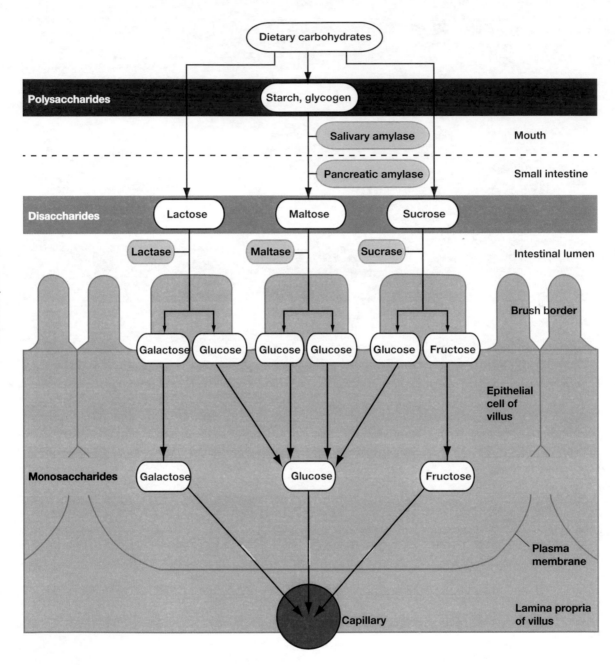

Figure 11.1: The process of carbohydrate digestion and absorption.

PROTEIN DIGESTION

Protein is the nutrient molecule found in meat, eggs, and legumes. Digestion of these very large amino acid polymers is begun in the stomach by **pepsin**. The process is completed in the small intestine with the help of a variety of **proteases** and **peptidases** (protein digesting enzymes) secreted by the pancreas and the brush border lining of the small intestine, as well as by enzymes found in the epithelial cells of the GI tract. **Trypsin** is a protease secreted by the pancreas and added to the small intestines. The substrate for this exercise is N-alpha-benzoyl-L-arginine-p-nitroanilide (BAPNA), a synthetic protein with a dye molecule attached to arginine, an amino acid. As BAPNA is digested, the dye is released and the solution becomes yellow.

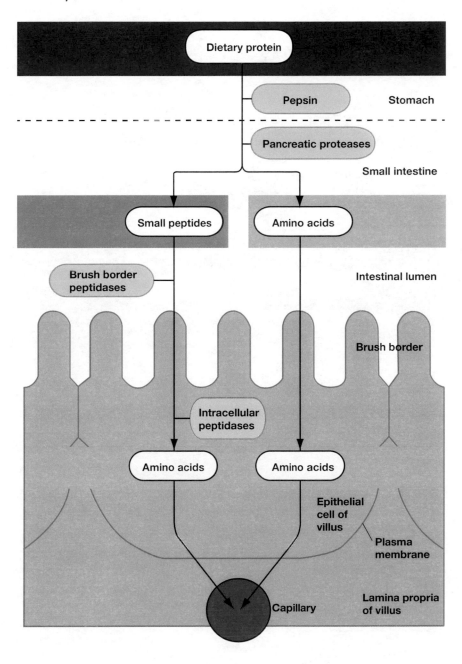

© bluedoor, LLC

Figure 11.2: The process of protein digestion and absorption.

FAT DIGESTION

Fats, such as vegetable oil, are **hydrophobic** and therefore don't mix with water. They form large globules in the watery environment of the digestive system. In this form, the fat molecules are not easily reached by **lipase**, the primary fat digesting enzyme. Therefore, **bile salts** from the liver are first mixed with these globules to disperse them into smaller droplets, a process called **emulsification**. This increases the surface area so that lipase can more efficiently digest the fats. Lipase is a pancreatic enzyme added to the small intestine. In this exercise you will use **pancreatin**, a solution of enzymes from the pancreas, including lipase. The fat substrate for this exercise is heavy cream. Litmus powder, a pH indicator, has been added to the whole cream in order to be able to use pH to assess digestion.

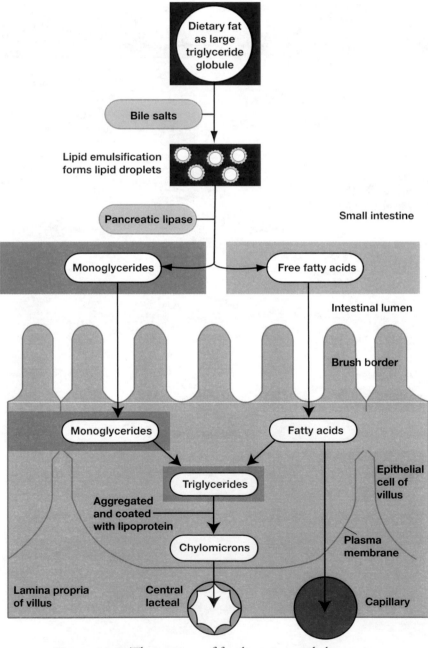

© bluedoor, LLC

Figure 11.3: The process of fat digestion and absorption.

Key Term Matching

_____ 1. BAPNA

_____ 2. mechanical digestion

_____ 3. lipase

_____ 4. fructose

_____ 5. monoglycerides + fatty acids

_____ 6. starch

_____ 7. chylomicrons

_____ 8. chemical digestion

_____ 9. pepsin

_____ 10. bile salts

_____ 11. lactose

_____ 12. monosaccharides

_____ 13. Lugol's solution

_____ 14. amylase

_____ 15. emulsification

_____ 16. protein

_____ 17. sucrose

_____ 18. trypsin

_____ 19. fats

_____ 20. maltose

_____ 21. Benedict's solution

_____ 22. pancreatin

_____ 23. galactose

_____ 24. litmus powder

_____ 25. amino acids

A. an enzyme that digests starch

B. molecules that are absorbed into the lacteals

C. enzyme that begins protein digestion in stomach

D. milk sugar

E. a substance that emulsifies fats

F. a solution that detects starch

G. a pH indicator

H. a monosaccharide found in sucrose

I. process of breaking fat globules into small droplets

J. table sugar

K. a polymer made of amino acids

L. a hydrophobic molecule

M. an example is grinding food with the teeth

N. an enzyme that digests fats

O. a protease secreted by the pancreas

P. a disaccharide containing two glucose molecules

Q. molecules that result from fat digestion

R. a solution that detects maltose

S. molecules that result from carbohydrate digestion

T. chemical reactions catalyzed by enzymes

U. a solution of enzymes from the pancreas

V. a synthetic protein

W. a monosaccharide found in lactose

X. molecules that result from protein digestion

Y. the primary dietary carbohydrate

Concept Map

▶ Use the word bank to fill in the blank spaces in each diagram.

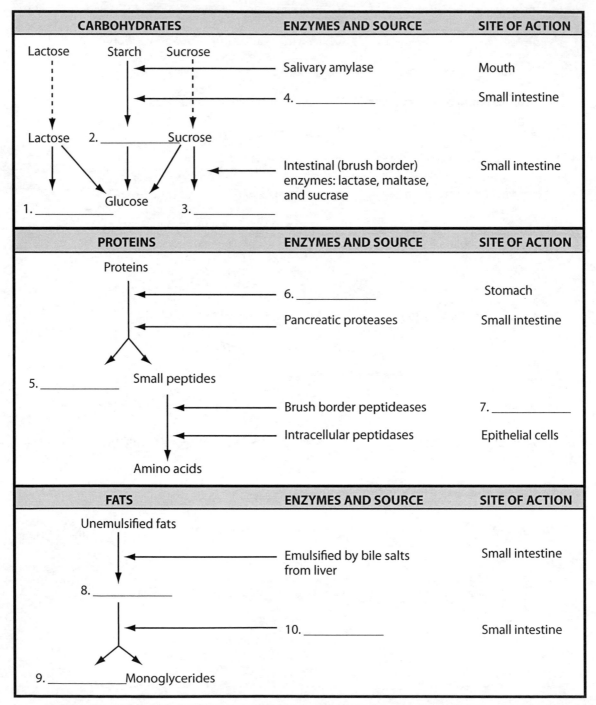

CARBOHYDRATES	ENZYMES AND SOURCE	SITE OF ACTION
Lactose Starch Sucrose	Salivary amylase	Mouth
	4. _____	Small intestine
Lactose 2. _____ Sucrose	Intestinal (brush border) enzymes: lactase, maltase, and sucrase	Small intestine
1. _____ Glucose 3. _____		

PROTEINS	ENZYMES AND SOURCE	SITE OF ACTION
Proteins	6. _____	Stomach
	Pancreatic proteases	Small intestine
5. _____ Small peptides		
	Brush border peptideases	7. _____
	Intracellular peptidases	Epithelial cells
Amino acids		

FATS	ENZYMES AND SOURCE	SITE OF ACTION
Unemulsified fats	Emulsified by bile salts from liver	Small intestine
8. _____		
	10. _____	Small intestine
9. _____ Monoglycerides		

Word Bank

amino acids	fructose	maltose	small intestine
emulsified fats	galactose	pancreatic amylase	
fatty acids	gastric pepsin	pancreatic lipase	

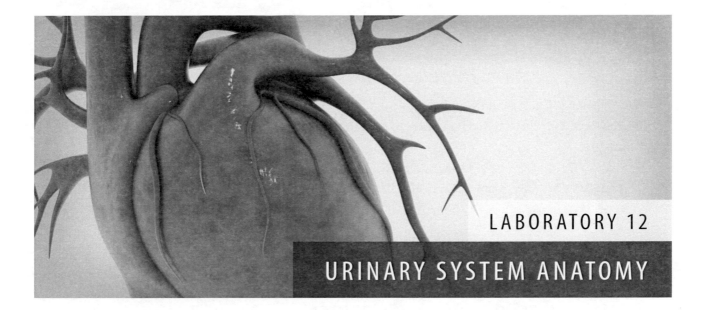

URINARY CALCULI

Urine contains many dissolved minerals, such as calcium oxalate, uric acid, calcium phosphate, and struvite (a mixture of magnesium, ammonium, and phosphate), that have been removed from the bloodstream. If the concentration of mineral salts is higher than can stay in solution, they begin to precipitate out of the urine, forming crystals. Normally these crystals are microscopic and are flushed away with the urine. However, under certain conditions these crystals begin to grow, forming **calculi** (commonly called stones) anywhere along the urinary tract.

Symptoms occur when large stones are unable to easily pass through the urinary system and include:

- pain — called **renal colic**
- obstruction of urine flow
- blood in the urine — called **hematuria** (*hemat-* means blood and *-uria* means urine condition)
- urinary tract infection (UTI)

Because stones are crystals, they are sharp and jagged. This causes pain and bleeding as the stone scrapes along the insides of the urinary tract. If a large stone becomes stuck, it physically blocks the free flow of urine. Urine may even back up all the way into the kidney, causing a condition called **hydronephrosis** (*hydro-* means water and *-nephrosis* means abnormal kidney condition). When urine flow is slow, bacteria begin to grow in areas behind the blockage, leading to the development of a UTI.

Calculi high up in the urinary tract can be broken up by a procedure called **extracorporeal shock wave lithotripsy** (ESWL). This procedure is non-invasive, meaning that there is no surgical incision. Rather, high-frequency sound waves are projected at the calculus, causing it to shatter. Then the pieces may pass through with the urine. Calculi in the lower parts of the urinary tract may be viewed endoscopically and broken up with a laser so that the pieces pass out with the urine.

Typically calculi form in the kidney, but not always. Calculi are named for the location at which they become lodged. The suffix *-lithiasis* means the condition of having stones.

- **Nephrolithiasis** is the condition of having stones in the kidney, usually lodged in the renal pelvis.
- **Ureterolithiasis** is the condition of having stones lodged in the ureter.
- **Cystolithiasis** is the condition of having stones lodged in the urinary bladder.

Any calculus that is able to fit through the internal urethral orifice is small enough to pass through the urethra. It is not typical to have a blockage in the urethra.

▶ For each condition listed below, indicate on the figure where each stone would be located. Then, for each stone location, list the structures which would contain backed up urine.

1. nephrolithiasis

2. ureterolithiasis

3. cystolithiasis

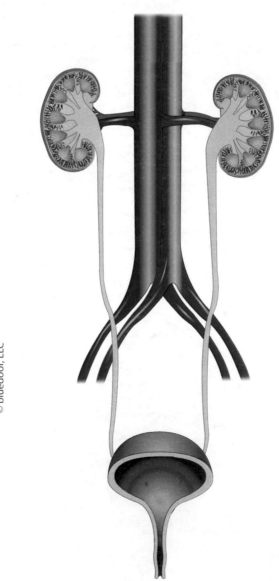

© bluedoor, LLC

Labeling Activity 1

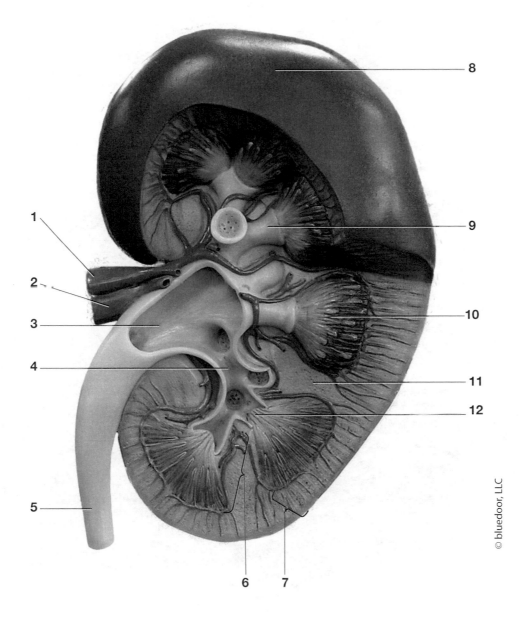

© bluedoor, LLC

1. _____   7. _____

2. _____   8. _____

3. _____   9. _____

4. _____   10. _____

5. _____   11. _____

6. _____   12. _____

Labeling Activity 2

1
(organ)

5

2

6

7

8

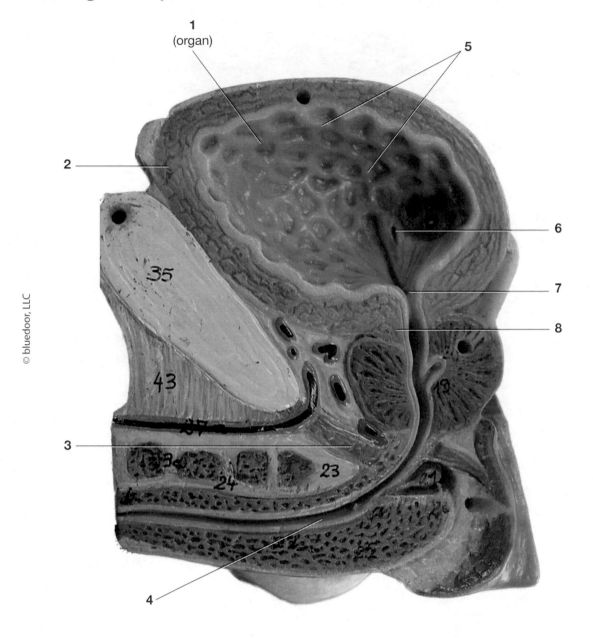

© bluedoor, LLC

3

4

1. _____   5. _____

2. _____   6. _____

3. _____   7. _____

4. _____   8. _____

Key Term Matching

_____ 1. kidney

_____ 2. vasa recta

_____ 3. renal column

_____ 4. rugae

_____ 5. medulla

_____ 6. ureter

_____ 7. renal vein

_____ 8. minor calyx

_____ 9. glomerulus

_____ 10. cortex

_____ 11. arcuate veins

_____ 12. major calyx

_____ 13. renal corpuscle

_____ 14. urinary bladder

_____ 15. detrusor muscle

_____ 16. hilum

_____ 17. renal papilla

_____ 18. segmental artery

_____ 19. renal pyramid

_____ 20. urethra

_____ 21. renal artery

_____ 22. external urethral sphincter

_____ 23. renal capsule

_____ 24. meatus

_____ 25. renal pelvis

A. transports urine from kidneys to urinary bladder

B. a ball-shaped capillary network

C. receives urine from a single renal papilla

D. travel along boundary between cortex and medulla

E. outer portion of the kidney

F. branch of the abdominal aorta

G. delivers urine to the renal pelvis

H. capillaries surrounding nephron loop

I. stores urine

J. area for renal vessels and ureter to enter/exit kidney

K. branch of the renal artery

L. area of kidney between renal pyramids

M. external opening of urethra

N. fibrous covering of the kidney

O. folds in the bladder wall

P. collects urine from major calyces

Q. composed of nephron loops and collecting ducts

R. composed of skeletal muscle

S. organ where nephrons are located

T. delivers blood to the inferior vena cava

U. inner portion of the kidney

V. wall of the urinary bladder

W. tip of a renal pyramid

X. composed of a glomerulus and glomerular capsule

Y. transports urine from bladder to the outside

Coloring Activity

Kidney

Major calyx

Minor calyx

Nephron

Renal artery

Renal capsule

Renal column

Renal cortex

Renal medulla

Renal pyramid

Renal vein

Renal pelvis

Ureter

Urethra

Urinary bladder

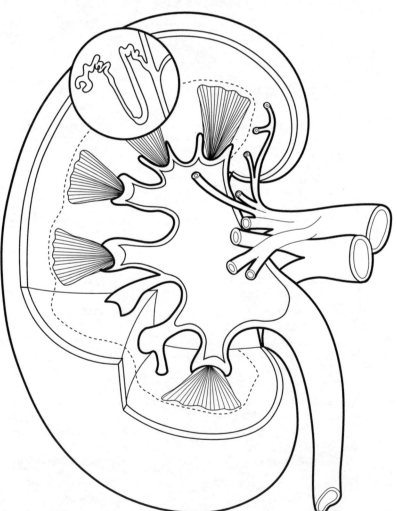

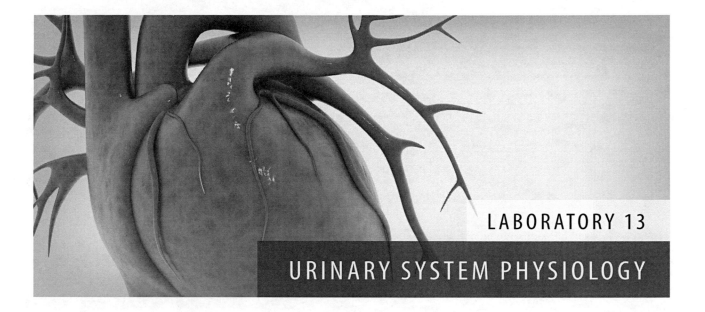

URINALYSIS

Physical Analysis

The physical characteristics of urine include its color, transparency, odor, pH, and specific gravity.

- **Color** – Normal urine colors range from pale yellow to amber, determined primarily by how dilute (pale yellow) or concentrated (amber) the urine is. Pathological colors include yellow-brown or green (caused by the presence of bile pigments) and red or dark brown (caused by the presence of blood).

- **Transparency** – Normal urine is clear to very slightly cloudy. Cloudy urine is the result of an increase in the amount of sediment present. This sediment could contain pus from bacterial infections.

- **Odor** – Normal urine has a highly characteristic odor described as "aromatic." Pathological urine specimens may have an ammonia smell caused by a bacterial infection or a fruity smell caused by the ketone bodies produced in a person with diabetes mellitus.

- **pH** – The normal range for urine pH is from 4.5 to 8.0. However, the average is slightly acidic, 6.0. Diet may affect pH in a non-pathological way. For example, foods high in protein increase acidity while a vegetarian diet increases alkalinity of the urine. Pathologically, a bacterial infection also raises the pH of the urine.

- **Specific gravity** – Specific gravity is a ratio of the weight of a specific volume of liquid compared to the weight of an equal volume of distilled water. Since 1 mL of distilled water weighs 1 g, its specific gravity is 1.000. Because urine contains dissolved substances, 1 mL of urine will weigh more than the distilled water. The specific gravity of normal urine is between 1.001 (if it is very dilute and clear) and 1.030 (if it is concentrated and slightly cloudy). In short, specific gravity is an indicator of the amount of solid particles suspended in the urine. Pathologically, urine that is more dilute that 1.001 may be the result of **diabetes insipidus**, an endocrine disease in which the body is unable to conserve water. Urine that is more concentrated than 1.030 may be the result of fever or a kidney infection called **pyelonephritis**.

Table 13.1: Abnormal Components of Urine.

Abnormal Component	Condition	Cause
Glucose	Glycosuria	Caused by glucose levels in the blood that exceed the renal tubule's ability to reabsorb it. It is a common sign of diabetes mellitus.
Albumin	Albuminuria	Caused by damage to the glomerular filtration membrane, resulting in the leakage of large proteins including albumin into the filtrate.
Red blood cells	Hematuria	Caused by damage to the glomerular filtration membrane, allowing whole cells from the blood to pass into the filtrate.
Hemoglobin	Hemoglobinuria	Caused by the hemolysis of red blood cells within the bloodstream, which releases hemoglobin into plasma and it crosses the glomerular filtration membrane during renal filtration. Diseases that cause red blood cell hemolysis include hemolytic anemia, glomerulonephritis, transfusion reactions, and burns.
Ketone bodies	Ketonuria	While very small levels in the urine are normal, higher levels are caused by abnormalities in metabolism as a result of enzyme deficiencies, starvation, or diets extremely low in carbohydrates, or diabetes mellitus.
White blood cells	Pyuria	Caused by inflammation of one or more organs of the urinary system, often as a reaction to infection.
Casts	Casts	A cast is a hardened cell fragment, caused by an abnormally low filtration rate, low pH, or high salt concentration of the filtrate.
Bacteria	Infection	Bacteria in the urine is a sign of a urinary tract infection, or UTI.

Labeling Activity 1

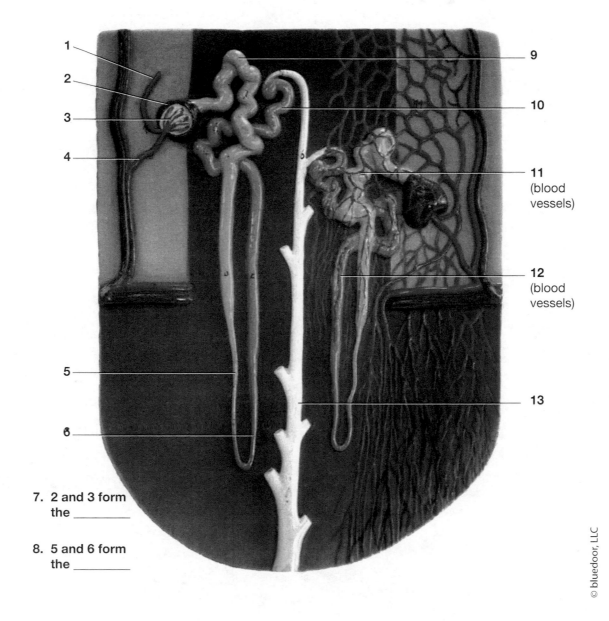

7. 2 and 3 form the _____

8. 5 and 6 form the _____

1. _____
2. _____
3. _____
4. _____
5. _____
6. _____
7. _____

8. _____
9. _____
10. _____
11. _____
12. _____
13. _____

Labeling Activity 2

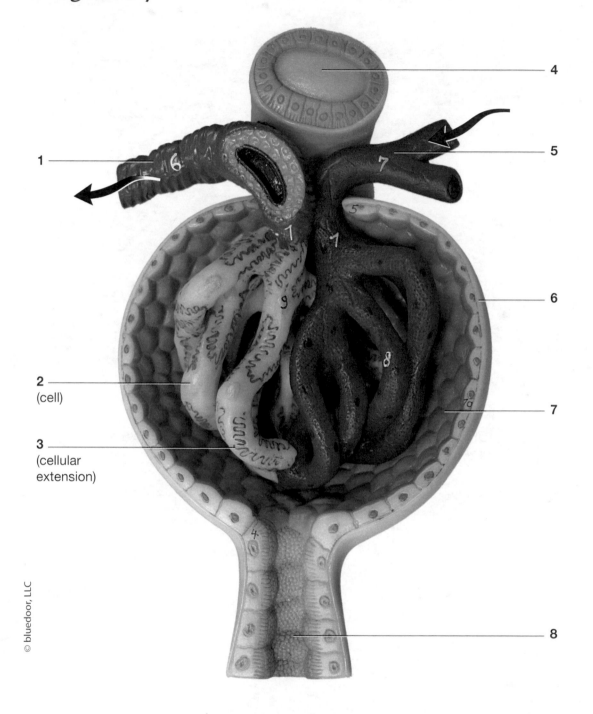

1 _____

2 _____
(cell)

3 _____
(cellular extension)

4 _____

5 _____

6 _____

7 _____

8 _____

1. _____   5. _____

2. _____   6. _____

3. _____   7. _____

4. _____   8. _____

Key Term Matching

_____ 1. podocyte

_____ 2. reabsorption

_____ 3. nephron

_____ 4. specific gravity

_____ 5. nephron loop

_____ 6. casts

_____ 7. efferent arteriole

_____ 8. pedicels

_____ 9. mesangial cells

_____ 10. vasa recta

_____ 11. filtration

_____ 12. proximal convoluted tubule

_____ 13. albuminuria

_____ 14. afferent arteriole

_____ 15. secretion

_____ 16. juxtaglomerular complex

_____ 17. hydrogen ion

_____ 18. peritubular capillaries

_____ 19. macula densa

_____ 20. filtration slit

_____ 21. glomerular capsule

_____ 22. sodium

_____ 23. distal convoluted tubule

_____ 24. ketone bodies

_____ 25. collecting duct

A. receives blood from the glomerulus

B. structure that secretes renin

C. extensions of the podocytes

D. condition of too much protein in the urine

E. blood vessels surrounding nephron loop

F. cells supporting the glomerular capillaries

G. receives filtrate from glomerular capsule

H. moves substances from renal tubules into capillaries

I. the functional unit of the kidney

J. a substance that undergoes secretion

K. blood vessels surrounding convoluted tubules

L. a substance that undergoes reabsorption

M. receives filtrate from glomerulus

N. houses pressure sensitive sensory receptors

O. part of a physical analysis of urine

P. delivers urine to the renal papilla

Q. a byproduct of fatty acid metabolism

R. delivers blood to the glomerulus

S. hardened, cylinder-shaped collection of cells

T. delivers urine to a collecting duct

U. allows filtrate to leave glomerular capillaries

V. moves substances from capillaries into renal tubules

W. has ascending and descending limbs

X. first stage of urine production

Y. cell forming inner wall of glomerular capsule

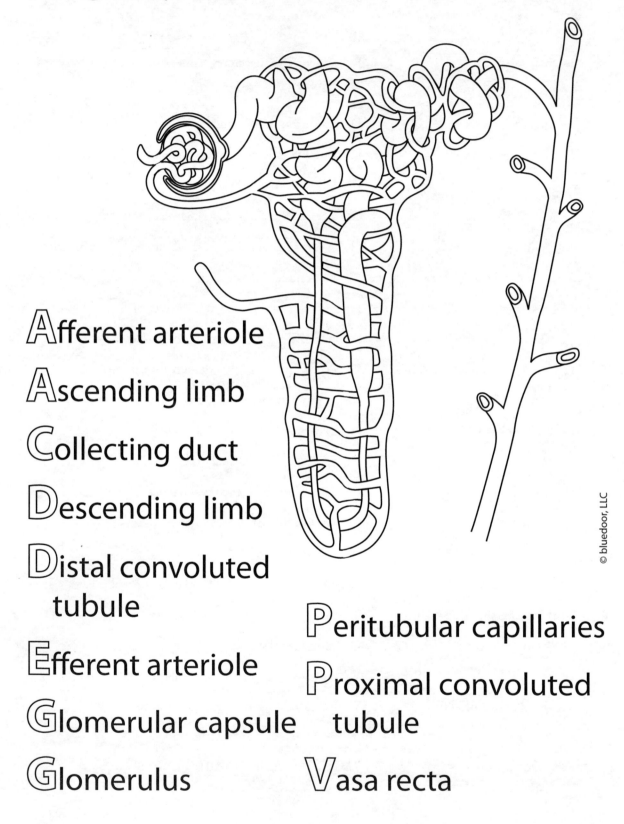

© bluedoor, LLC

Afferent arteriole

Ascending limb

Collecting duct

Descending limb

Distal convoluted
  tubule

Efferent arteriole

Glomerular capsule

Glomerulus

Peritubular capillaries

Proximal convoluted
  tubule

Vasa recta

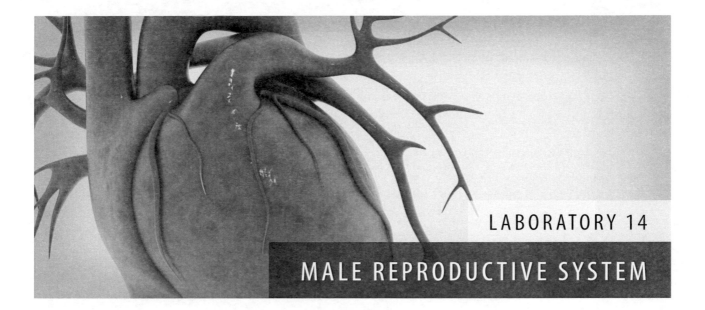

TESTICULAR PATHOLOGIES

Several pathologies involving the testes, epididymides, and spermatic cord are described below. They are then illustrated on the next page. The challenge is to read about each pathology and then correctly match the name to the illustration.

Cryptorchidism: During fetal development, the testes form in the pelvic cavity. Then, shortly before birth, they descend into the normal position within the scrotum. Cryptorchidism means that the migration from pelvic cavity to scrotum fails to occur for either one or both testes. If the condition does not correct itself by age 2, then a surgical procedure is performed, called **orchiopexy**, to correctly position the testes.

Epididymitis: Epididymitis is swelling and inflammation of the epididymis. It is frequently the result of an infection spreading from the urethra into the epididymis. Symptoms include pain and tenderness in the scrotum and blood in the semen.

Hydrocele: This condition occurs when excess fluid escapes from the peritoneal cavity and collects in the cavity between the two layers of the tunica vaginalis. When this condition exists at birth, it typically corrects itself and the excess fluid is reabsorbed. The primary symptom is a painless, swollen scrotum that feels like a water balloon.

Orchitis: Orchitis is pain and swelling in one or both testes. It may be caused by a variety of bacteria and viruses. It is a potential complication of mumps and can result in infertility by damaging the testes. It may also be associated with infections of the prostate gland or epididymis. Symptoms include pain and swelling in the scrotum and blood in the semen.

Spermatic cord varicocele: A varicocele is a dilated vein. In this case, it is one of the veins in the spermatic cord. It typically develops after puberty and is caused by too few valves in the vein, allowing blood to pool. When this condition is mild it is usually pain free. If the condition is severe, then there is tenderness and the possibility of infertility. Infertility may be due to the impaired flow to the testicles and the increased testicular temperature. Spermatogenesis is a temperature-dependent process. If there is increased flow of warm blood to the testes, then their internal temperature may be increased.

Testicular torsion: Testicular torsion is caused by a twisting of the spermatic cord, which threatens to cut off blood supply to the testes if not quickly corrected. This condition may develop as the result of testicular trauma, but some men are congenitally prone to the condition because they have insufficient connective tissue surrounding and protecting the blood vessels in the spermatic cord.

▶ Use the terms in the Word Bank to label each pathology.

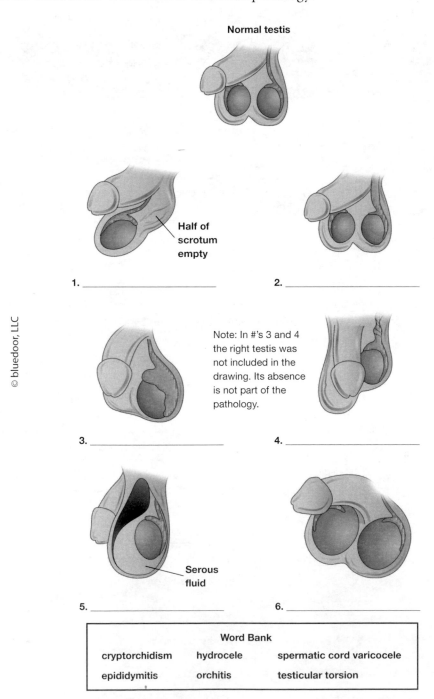

Normal testis

Half of scrotum empty

1. _____   2. _____

Note: In #'s 3 and 4 the right testis was not included in the drawing. Its absence is not part of the pathology.

3. _____   4. _____

Serous fluid

5. _____   6. _____

Word Bank		
cryptorchidism	hydrocele	spermatic cord varicocele
epididymitis	orchitis	testicular torsion

© bluedoor, LLC

Labeling Activity 1

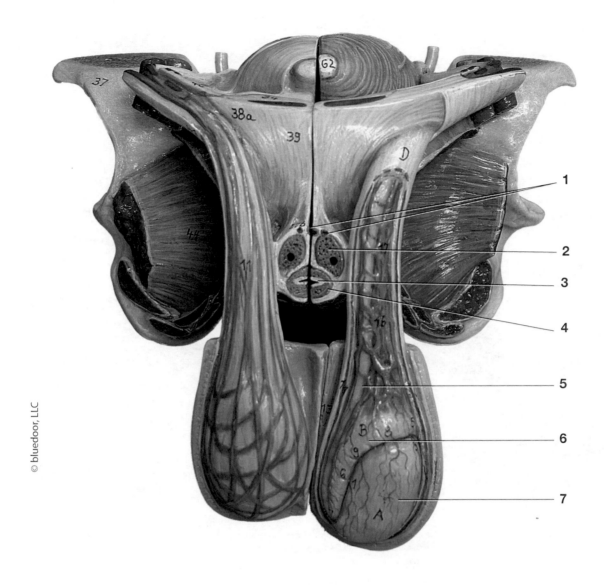

1. _____   5. _____

2. _____   6. _____

3. _____   7. _____

4. _____

Labeling Activity 2

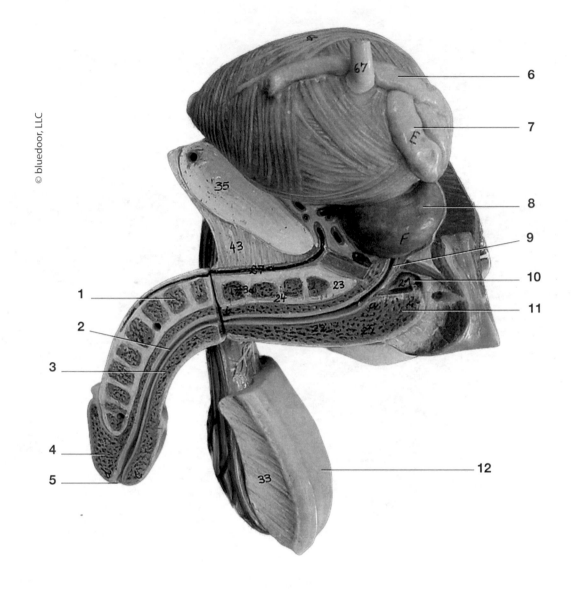

1. _____   7. _____

2. _____   8. _____

3. _____   9. _____

4. _____   10. _____

5. _____   11. _____

6. _____   12. _____

Key Term Matching

_____1. semen

_____2. spermatogenesis

_____3. rete testis

_____4. secondary spermatocyte

_____5. interstitial cell

_____6. testis

_____7. sperm midpiece

_____8. bulbourethral gland

_____9. seminal vesicles

_____10. scrotum

_____11. tunica albuginea

_____12. acrosomal cap

_____13. sperm

_____14. spermatid

_____15. prostate gland

_____16. spermiogenesis

_____17. Sertoli cell

_____18. spermatic cord

_____19. spermatogonium

_____20. primary spermatocyte

_____21. epididymis

_____22. prepuce

_____23. seminiferous tubule

_____24. corpus spongiosum

_____25. ampulla

A. a cell that has completed meiosis II

B. the male gonad

C. contains mitochondria in spiral formation

D. network of tubules between testis and epididymis

E. commonly called the foreskin

F. site of sperm storage and maturation

G. secrete 60% of fluid in semen

H. accessory gland encircling urethra

I. white fibrous capsule around testis

J. column of erectile tissue

K. consists of sperm and fluid from accessory glands

L. also called a nurse cell

M. spermatogenesis occurs within its wall

N. diploid stem cell

O. a cell that has completed meiosis I

P. consists of ductus deferens, vessels, and nerves

Q. widened terminal end of ductus deferens

R. also called Cowper's gland

S. a cell entering spermatogenesis

T. the male gamete

U. meiosis process that produces sperm

V. contains enzymes vital for fertilization

W. skin sac encasing testes and epididymides

X. secretes testosterone

Y. physical change of spermatid to sperm

Coloring Activity

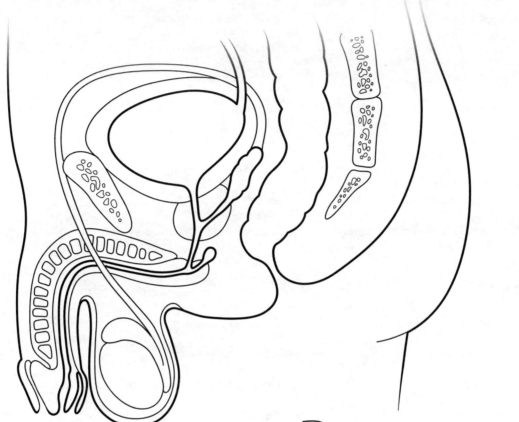

Bulbourethral gland

Corpus cavernosum

Corpus spongiosum

Ductus deferens

Epididymis

Glans penis

Membranous urethra

Penile urethra

Prepuce

Prostate gland

Prostatic urethra

Scrotum

Seminal vesicle

Shaft of penis

Testis

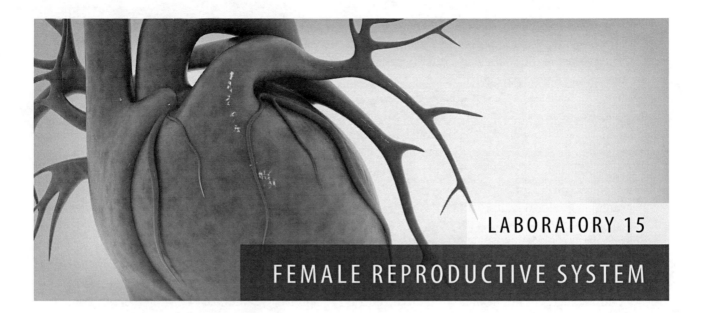

CONTRACEPTION

Because the reproductive process is complex with multiple steps, there are several different strategies for contraception. Each one interferes with a specific step in the process.

Abstinence — The avoidance of sexual intercourse.

Rhythm method — Refraining from sexual intercourse during the time around ovulation. This method is effective only if the woman has regular menstrual cycles so that ovulation can be correctly anticipated.

Coitus interruptus — The withdrawal of the penis from the vagina prior to ejaculation.

Condom — A latex or lambskin sheath placed over the erect penis to prevent semen from being deposited in the vagina.

Diaphragm with **spermicide** — A rubber dome-shaped covering that is placed over the cervix. Prevents sperm in the vagina from entering the uterus. Use of a diaphragm is typically paired with a spermicide applied on the cervical side of the diaphragm. A spermicide is a chemical that will kill any sperm that make their way around the edges of the diaphragm.

Vasectomy — An outpatient procedure during which a small section of each ductus (vas) deferens is removed through a small incision in the scrotum. The cut ends of the ductus deferens are tied off. This does not interfere with spermatogenesis but prevents sperm from traveling through the ductus deferens. Semen will contain only secretions from male reproductive glands.

Tubal ligation — A major surgical procedure during which a small section of each uterine tube is surgically removed and the cut ends are tied off. This prevents sperm in one side of the uterine tube from reaching the ovum in the other side.

Birth control pill, patch, shot, implant — These are all examples of hormonal contraception containing either a combination of estrogen and progestin (a substance similar to progesterone) or just progestin. They prevent either oogenesis (by preventing follicle development) or ovulation, depending on the particular brand.

Intrauterine device (IUD) — A flexible, plastic T-shaped device is placed inside the uterus by a physician. How it works is not clearly understood, but it is thought to alter the endometrium so that the chances of a fertilized ovum implanting are significantly reduced.

Emergency contraception (morning-after pill) — These pills contain a higher level of progestin than found in birth control pills. The three effects of taking progestin at this level are: prevention of ovulation, thickening of the cervical mucus (which blocks sperm from entering uterus), and prevention of implantation by thinning the endometrial lining.

Induced abortion — The term abortion means the ending of a pregnancy. A spontaneous abortion is a miscarriage. An intentional or induced abortion to remove the embryo may be performed surgically or chemically.

Below is a flow diagram outlining the events necessary to produce a baby. Contraceptive methods affect different steps along this process. Use the terms provided in the Word Bank to indicate where each contraceptive method has its effects. Note that it is possible to use a term more than once.

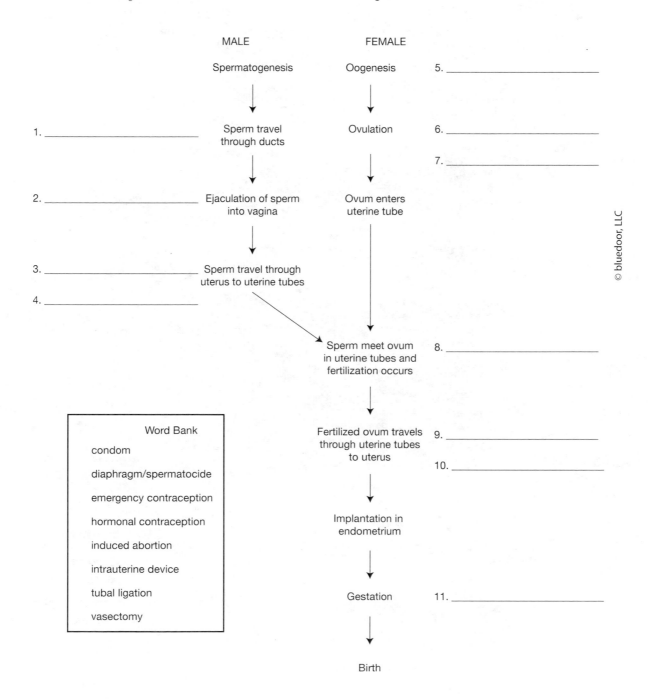

MALE   FEMALE

Spermatogenesis   Oogenesis   5. _____

1. _____ Sperm travel through ducts   Ovulation   6. _____

                                          7. _____

2. _____ Ejaculation of sperm into vagina   Ovum enters uterine tube

3. _____ Sperm travel through uterus to uterine tubes

4. _____

Sperm meet ovum in uterine tubes and fertilization occurs   8. _____

Fertilized ovum travels through uterine tubes to uterus   9. _____

                                        10. _____

Implantation in endometrium

Word Bank

condom

diaphragm/spermatocide

emergency contraception

hormonal contraception

induced abortion

intrauterine device

tubal ligation

vasectomy

Gestation   11. _____

Birth

Labeling Activity 1

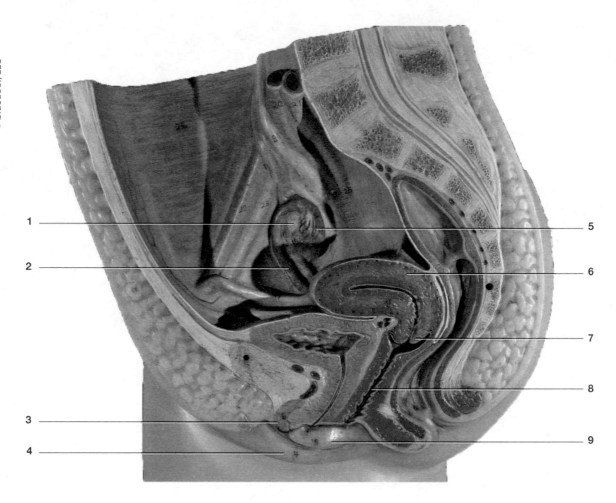

1. _____
2. _____
3. _____
4. _____
5. _____

6. _____
7. _____
8. _____
9. _____

Labeling Activity 2

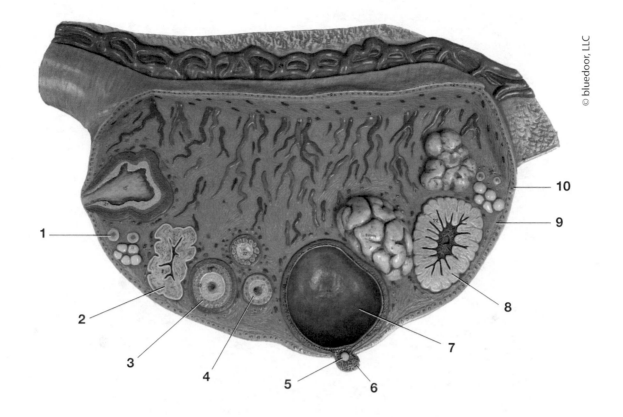

1. _____   6. _____

2. _____   7. _____

3. _____   8. _____

4. _____   9. _____

5. _____   10. _____

Key Term Matching

_____ 1. ovaries

_____ 2. corpus albicans

_____ 3. primordial follicles

_____ 4. germinal epithelium

_____ 5. vulva

_____ 6. vestibule

_____ 7. uterine tubes

_____ 8. antrum

_____ 9. uterus

_____ 10. endometrium

_____ 11. fundus

_____ 12. corona radiata

_____ 13. secretory alveoli

_____ 14. vagina

_____ 15. lactation

_____ 16. granulosa cells

_____ 17. fimbriae

_____ 18. nipple

_____ 19. myometrium

_____ 20. clitoris

_____ 21. areola

_____ 22. cervical os

_____ 23. cervix

_____ 24. ovulation

_____ 25. hymen

A. dome-shaped region of uterus

B. release of secondary oocyte into pelvic cavity

C. typical site of fertilization

D. scar tissue remnant of corpus luteum

E. provides place for fetal development

F. opening through cervix

G. form multiple layers in follicle wall

H. produce milk

I. inner lining of uterus

J. the female gonad

K. follicle cells around oocyte in tertiary follicle

L. partially blocks vaginal orifice

M. finger-like extensions of uterine tubes

N. the muscular layer of the uterus

O. contains erectile tissue

P. the process of producing milk

Q. the outer covering of the ovaries

R. the external genitalia

S. conical-shaped projection of breast

T. inferior portion of uterus

U. open space created by labia minora

V. found in clusters called the egg nest

W. reddish-brown skin around nipple

X. pocket of fluid that forms in secondary follicle

Y. receives penis during intercourse

Coloring Activity

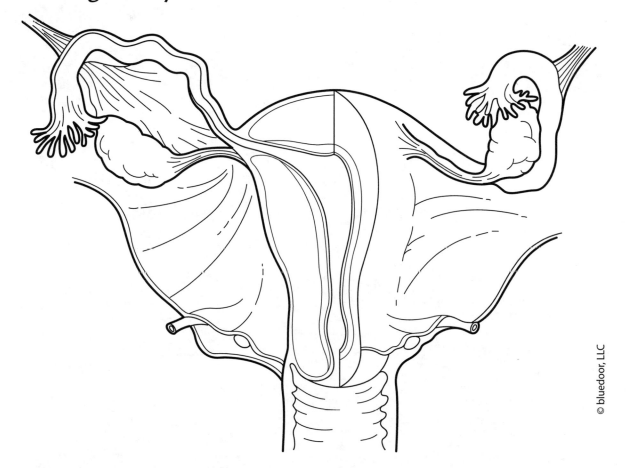

Broad ligament

Cervix of uterus

Endometrium

Fimbriae

Infundibulum

Myometrium

Ovarian ligament

Ovary

Perimetrium

Suspensory ligament

Uterine cavity

Uterine tube

Vagina